Free Stuff
for Baby!

Free Stuff
for Baby!

*The New Parents' Ultimate Guide to
Hundreds of Dollars of Baby Freebies
and Parenting Resources*

Sue M. Hannah

Contemporary Books

Chicago   New York   San Francisco   Lisbon   London   Madrid   Mexico City
Milan   New Delhi   San Juan   Seoul   Singapore   Sydney   Toronto

Library of Congress Cataloging-in-Publication Data

Hannah, Sue M.
    Free stuff for baby! : the new parents' ultimate guide to hundreds of dollars
of baby freebies and parenting resources / Sue M. Hannah.
        p.   cm.
    ISBN 0-07-141009-0
    1. Infants' supplies industry—Directories.   2. Free material—Directories.
I. Title.

HD9970.5.I542 H36   2003
649'.122'0297—dc21   2002034795

3 4 5 6 7 8 9 0   DOC/DOC   2 1 0 9 8 7 6 5 4 3

ISBN 0-07-141009-0

Interior design by Amy Yu Ng

McGraw-Hill books are available at special quantity discounts to use as premiums and sales promotions, or for use in corporate training programs. For more information, please write to the Director of Special Sales, Professional Publishing, McGraw-Hill, Two Penn Plaza, New York, NY 10121-2298. Or contact your local bookstore.

This book is printed on acid-free paper.

To Kayla, Shane, and Katie

You have opened up my world with your imagination.

You fill my heart with love. You are my blessings!

Contents

Acknowledgments

Writing this book has been a wonderful experience but definitely a challenge at times. I couldn't have done it without the support and encouragement from many wonderful people, whose names I would like to mention at this time:

A very special thanks to my editors, Betsy Lancefield Lane and Denise Betts at Contemporary Books/McGraw-Hill. Thanks for believing in me and giving me this wonderful opportunity!

Many thanks to Catherine McDiarmid and all who contributed their wonderful frugal baby tips at the Born to Love website.

Cindy Rehberg, my research assistance

Pat Neuman, Welcome Wagon

American Academy of Pediatrics

Canadian Paediatric Society

U.S. Consumer Product Safety Commission

To my mom and dad

It's so comforting to know that you are always there for me and support me in everything that I do. Through you I have learned to appreciate the simple things in life, the things that are truly important, like spending quality time together and just being there for each other through the good and the bad. Thanks for being there for me every step of the way!

No thanks would be complete without mentioning my never-ending support team of friends, family, and relatives:

Don, Cameron, and Amanda Herzberg; Pete, Rebecca, Ashley, and Julia Herzberg; and Paul, Kelly, and Alexandria Moffat.

To the doting grandparents, Joan and Al MacDonald, who have spoiled my kids rotten!

Diane Jacques and family

Janine Green and family

Thank you so much for your help and support at a time when I really needed it. You're the best.

To my husband

Thanks for playing Super Dad to our three children while I locked myself away in the basement working on this book. (I am truly sorry for the time I missed out with all of you). Thanks for believing in me. I never could have done it without you.

To Kayla, Shane, and Katie

I often hear parents talk about their child's first step or their child's first words, and as truly precious as those things are, I've always felt that it is the little things that have melted my heart time and time again, the little day-to-day experiences that take you away from whatever it is that you are doing at the time—the way your faces light up when I walk into the room, the way you run to me in a crowd of strangers, the way you are consoled by my kisses, or even more delicious, the first time you gave me a big kiss and a hug and said, "I love you, Mommy." Those are the sweet memories that will remain in my heart forever.

Love you all! God bless.

Introduction

One of the few times that you will find companies eager to hand you free things is when you're having a baby. Many new or expecting parents do not know how easy it is to get a free sample or discount on their favorite items. Did you know that many well-known companies give free samples, coupons, and other terrific promotional items for many child care items? It's true! These products are free for the asking. All you have to do is call them (many have toll-free numbers), apply online at their websites, or write to them simply asking them to send you these valuable items.

Yes, You Can Get Something for Nothing!

First of all, if you are a new or expecting mom, congratulations and best wishes. This is a very special time for you, a time you will always cherish.

When I first found out that I was pregnant with my now 1½-year-old twins, Shane and Katie, I felt really excited and blessed to be having two babies and could hardly wait for their arrival. Also at the time being the mother of a 2½-year-old, Kayla, I realized from experience that there could be a significant financial strain when a new child enters the family.

So as the expectant mother of twins, I was desperate to get some financial help for my family, especially after being taken aback by a recent article I had read in a parenting magazine. This article plainly stated the staggering costs involved in raising a child. I was astonished to learn that the average parent will probably spend more than $1,500 on premium disposable diapers by the time a child is potty-trained. With twins on the way, I did some quick calculations in my head, multiplied those figures by two, took a deep breath, and realized that, yes, we really did need some extra help.

After carefully going over the family budget with my husband and deciding on some general cutbacks (e.g., pay-TV, the *TV Guide*, subscriptions to those glossy women's magazines that I just loved to read, book club memberships, and just about everything else we could think of), we still came up short.

I subsequently sat down and tried to think of ways to get a little more help for my family. I spent several hours surfing the Internet, reading through parenting magazines and parenting guides, visiting local department stores, as well as making several calls to different companies that offered baby products to find out what kind of help was out there for new or expecting moms.

Many hours and several phone calls later, I was truly surprised to find that so many companies offered free products or samples to new or expecting moms who contacted them by simply making a toll-free phone call, writing a letter, or applying online—and with no obligation to buy anything! These companies were eager to respond to my requests for free samples and promotional products, and in a couple of weeks my mailbox was flooded with valuable free stuff. I could hardly wait to see what my mailman brought me in the mail each day. I received free gift packs, parenting starter kits, coupons, parenting books and magazines, and tons of samples in the mail. I got samples of almost every brand of diaper and formula on the market, plus I received many free gift items for my babies, including baby bibs, bottles, rattles, and much, much more. (One year later I am still receiving free promotional items in the mail!)

Thanks to these truly generous companies, I have had the luxury of freely sampling brand-name products without having to spend my hard-earned money testing out product after product, trying to find the best ones for my babies. I feel much more prepared and can make informed choices on the types of products that my babies will use—and I have truly loved spoiling my babies with all of these great products.

This book will introduce you to tons of companies that offer free samples and other great products for you or your baby. These free offers not only will save you tons of money but will give you the opportunity to compare different brands of baby products and choose only the best ones for your baby.

The extensive list of free parenting books, magazines, and other literature is available to educate you on every topic of parenting. The support groups are there for you, simply by calling a toll-free number, when you have a parenting question or concern, or even if you just need someone to talk to. In Chapter 11, "Ways to Stretch Your Dollar," you will learn of practical and simple ways to save even more money. Be sure to check out "My Top-Ten List of Totally Useless Baby Items" in Chapter 12 for some infant unnecessaries, things you can definitely do without. Chapter 7, "Free Government Resources for New or Expecting Parents," is an extremely valuable section, one that all parents should be made aware of. It will direct you to government programs that offer free financial assistance to low- and middle-income families, programs that provide free nutritious foods to needy families, a listing of available tax credits for new or expecting parents, information on how you can receive free health insurance and medical assistance, free government publications, and various other government assistance programs. This section also outlines maternity and parental benefits and what your rights and entitlements are as a new or expecting parent. While you're spoiling your new baby with all sorts of fabulous freebies, don't forget to "baby" yourself—because you deserve a break! Check out Chapter 10, "Mom's Free Stuff," where you can find out where to get some luxurious freebies, just for you, such as free perfume samples, cosmetic and hair samples, and more. Join as many mailing lists as you can and take advantage of what various companies have to offer.

The freebies in this book really help and can go a long way, but there are other things you can give to your new baby as well: lots of love, hugs, kisses, and cuddles. These are truly the most important things that you can offer your baby—and they're free, too!

Enjoy your free stuff!

Remember

Babies are little for such a short period of time, and for that time, you, as parents, are the center of their universe, the most important people in the world to them—you rock their world!

It gives me such great pleasure and pride to be a mom to my three beautiful children, Kayla, 4, and twins Shane and Katie, 1½ years of age. I am so very grateful to be that special person in their lives.

Enjoy your baby. Cherish every moment!

How the Book Works

The lists that I have compiled for you consist of companies that offer free samples and other great products to residents of the United States and Canada.

About 95 percent of the offers listed in this book are absolutely free, with no strings attached. There are, however, a few listings that, while free, require you to pay a small shipping and handling fee and/or send a self-addressed, stamped envelope, which the company can use to mail the product back to you. (The cost of the stamp is well worth it!)

When calling or writing to these companies, ask to be placed on their mailing lists for any promotional items, special benefits, or coupons and samples for new or expecting moms. Be prepared to state the due date of your baby. You can register with most of these companies right away, but with some of the companies you may have to wait until your baby is born to register. Some of the companies listed will offer free products and samples only until your baby reaches 6 months of age, so be sure to register as early as you can. Some companies may require a copy of the infant's birth certificate or a copy of the newspaper announcement. Be sure to send a photocopy only, not the original.

Unless advised otherwise, address all inquiries "Attn: Customer Service," and be sure to print your complete contact information (including your name, street and/or E-mail address, and phone number) in any request that you make to these companies. It might also be a good idea to state the sex of your baby.

Many of the companies listed throughout this book have a multiple-birth program available where they will send two, three, or four times the coupons and free samples for moms who are expecting twins, triplets, quadruplets, or higher. Be sure to state that you are expecting multiples in your telephone conversation or letter to each company you contact.

Once you've received your freebies, you may wish to take the time to drop a quick thank-you note in the mail to all responding companies to show your appreciation.

Online Updates for Your Added Convenience

In my quest to keep this book as up-to-date as possible, I have created a website (www.freestuff4baby.com) where readers can go to find postings on the latest and most current company offers. Included on this website will be postings of new offers that have been made available since I wrote this book and offers that have been discontinued, as well as general changes in company information, including address changes and other pertinent changes in contact information. Please feel free to visit my website and browse around.

Have you found any offers that have discontinued or changed? Have any of the companies listed in this book changed their toll-free numbers or addresses? Has your request been returned to you for any reason? Please drop me an E-mail (sue@freestuff4baby.com) or write to me at the address provided to let me know—and to tell me what you think of the book. Feel free to send any comments or suggestions you might have. I would love to hear from you. Thanks!

Sue Hannah
P.O. Box 23026
Westgate Postal Outlet
Cambridge, ON N1S 4Z6
Canada

Disclaimer

Despite my best effort to make the information in this book as timely and accurate as possible, there are bound to be listings that will be outdated by the time it reaches your hands. Companies may change their promotional offers from time to time, and you may not always receive the freebies that are listed in this book. Companies may move and change their mailing information and phone numbers. Supplies of some items may be limited.

The companies listed in this book have the right to discontinue or substitute their offers at any time they wish. Their offers are subject to change without notice. If the item or publication you are inquiring about is no longer available, ask if the company has anything new or if the item will be offered at a later time. Be sure to check back again as companies will often bring an offer back at a later time—or may offer an even newer and better free promotional item!

Please be advised that the publisher cannot be held responsible if you do not receive any particular free item listed in this book or if you receive an item that is different from what has been listed in the book. Do not contact the publisher of this book about unfilled or improperly filled orders.

In fairness to our readers, we have not received payment from any of the companies so they could be listed in this book or could receive a better placement in this book. All companies have been treated equally and are simply listed in alphabetical order for your convenience.

Free Stuff
for Baby!

Baby Freebies Delivered to Your Door

This chapter contains tons of toll-free numbers and company names that parents can call or write to receive free stuff for their baby, including free diapers, baby wipes, formula, bibs and rattles, gift packs and parenting starter kits, gift certificates and coupons, baby food samples, additional freebies for parents of multiples, and much, much more! Join as many mailing lists as you can. Be sure to join early in your pregnancy, or when your baby first arrives, to be sure to get the most benefit from these companies.

American Baby

www.americanbaby.com (click on "Free Offers")

American Baby offers a free gift basket to all new or expectant moms! These gift baskets contain various baby freebies, samples, coupons, and more and are available through your hospital or childbirth educator. If you don't receive your free basket at the hospital where you will be giving birth to your baby, be sure to ask your nurse or other hospital staff about the free American Baby Basket for new or expectant mothers. This offer is available to residents of the United States and at participating hospitals only.

The website's "Free Offers and More!" area features three types of offers:

Free: products and services for baby
Save: special savings on products you use every day
Win: everything from a year's worth of formula to an entire
wardrobe for baby

Plus, the monthly "Free Offers" E-mail newsletter delivers these special offers right to you! Check out the website for details.

❦ Ansa Bottle Company

1200 South Main
Muskogee, OK 74402
In the United States or Canada, call 918-687-1664 (sorry, not a toll-free number)

Ansa Bottle Company offers a free case of baby bottles to parents of quadruplets. Write or call for details.

❦ Associated Hygienic Products (Drypers)

P.O. Box 8830
Vancouver, WA 98666-8830
In the United States or Canada, call 888-639-5863
www.drypers.com

Write to Drypers and send a copy of your baby's birth certificate or birth announcement, plus return mailing information, to receive free Drypers diaper packages and coupons. Call for further details.

This company has a multiple-birth program for parents of twins, triplets, quadruplets, or higher. Drypers will send you one coupon for a free package of Drypers diapers for each child, as well as discount coupons. Parents of multiples can write to the attention of the Drypers multiple-birth program, sending copies of their babies' birth certificates or birth announcement, plus return mailing information.

These offers are available to residents of the United States and Canada.

❧ Babies "R" Us

In the United States, call 800-543-7787

www.babiesrus.com (click on "Baby Registry" under "Gifts and
   Registries")

Call to be added to the Kids "R" Us, Toys "R" Us, and Babies "R" Us mailing list to receive free coupons, as well as a catalog twice a year from Babies "R" Us. This offer is available to residents of the United States only.

Babies "R" Us and Toys "R" Us also have a baby registry where you can register for your baby shower. Visit a Babies "R" Us or Toys "R" Us store or go online to register. (See "Drop-In Freebies" in Chapter 3, "Free Stuff from Stores," for further details.)

❧ Babymil and Babysoy Formula

See PBM Products, Inc.

❧ Baby Orajel

See Del Laboratories.

❧ Beech-Nut Nutrition Corporation

Attn: Promotions

100 South Fourth Street

Suite 1010

St. Louis, MO 63102

In the United States or Canada, call 800-233-2468

www.beech-nut.com (click on "Coupons and Special Offers")

Call or write to receive a free New Parents Pack, with coupons for baby food and baby cereal. The Beech-Nut website also offers discount coupons that you can print out for further savings. See the website for details. This offer is available to residents of the United States.

Call to obtain information on Beech-Nut's label-saving program, where you can collect and send in proof-of-purchase labels to receive coupons for baby food. The label-saving program is available to residents of the United States only.

Residents of Canada can call to receive a free thirty-two-page nutrition information booklet with feeding guidelines from Beech-Nut.

This company has a multiple-birth program for parents of twins, triplets, quadruplets, or higher. Ask for details.

❧ *Best Wishes* (Canada's Baby Magazine)

The Best Wishes package is presented to new mothers after they give birth. The package includes *Best Wishes*, Canada's baby magazine, together with a great assortment of free samples and coupons. You should receive your package at the hospital or through other health care personnel after you give birth to your baby. Ask at the hospital where you will be giving birth about the free Best Wishes package for new or expecting mothers. This offer is available to residents of Canada and at participating hospitals only.

❧ Care Net

In the United States and Canada, call 800-395-HELP
www.care-net.org

Care Net is a twenty-four-hour, toll-free help line that supports more than 600 pregnancy centers across the United States and Canada. You can call Care Net with your pregnancy-related questions and concerns or to receive practical assistance and support. Care Net will refer you to the pregnancy center nearest you. Residents of the United States and Canada can call Care Net to receive a pregnancy test, free of charge.

❧ Carter's

The William Carter Company
Attn: Multiple Birth Program
224 North Hill Street

Griffin, GA 30223
In the United States or Canada, call 800-241-5066
www.carters.com

Carter's has a multiple-birth program for parents of triplets only. Please send copies of your babies' birth certificates to Carter's to receive free Carter's clothing for your babies. Be sure to state the sex of your babies in your written request. This offer is available to residents of the United States and Canada.

Catalina Lighting
Attn: Consumer Service Department
18191 Northwest 68 Avenue
Miami, FL 33015
In the United States or Canada, call 800-985-2220
www.catalinalighting.com

To receive a free halogen bulb cover safety kit to protect your child from burns, mail a request to Catalina Lighting. In your request, indicate how many kits you require, together with your mailing information. You should allow four to six weeks for delivery. This offer is available to residents of the United States and Canada.

Child Safety Seat Program
See State of Virginia.

DaimlerChrysler
In the United States, call 877-FIT-4-AKID (Fitting Station Locator)
www.fitforakid.org

More than 80 percent of children are incorrectly restrained in child seats, or the seats are not properly secured in the car. As a result, millions of children are at risk. The Fit for a Kid Program has trained inspectors to help you install your child seats the right way. No matter what kind of car you drive, you can make an appointment at a participating

DaimlerChrysler dealer for a free child safety seat inspection, as well as to receive information on car seat safety. Help is available, free of charge, by phone appointment. Call or go online to find the dealer nearest you. This offer is available to residents of the United States only.

❦ Dairy Farmers of Canada
In Canada, call 800-361-4632

Dairy Farmers of Canada offers a free Canada Food Guide Breast-feeding Chart to new or expecting moms. When you call, ask for the order desk to place your order. This offer is available to residents of Canada only.

❦ Del Laboratories (Baby Orajel)
In the United States or Canada, call 800-952-5080
www.orajel.com/baby/baby.html

Call to be put on Baby Orajel's mailing list to receive free coupons and information on Baby Orajel, or fill out the online survey to receive valuable discount coupons and rebates for toothache, teething, and oral care products. This offer is available to residents of the United States and Canada.

❦ Diaper Genie
See Playtex Products, Inc.

❦ Drypers
See Associated Hygienic Products.

❦ Earth's Best Baby Food
See Hain Celestial Group, Inc.

❦ Evenflo Company, Inc.
Attn: Multiple Birth Program

1801 Commerce Drive

Piqua, OH 45356

In the United States, call 800-356-BABY

In Canada, call 800-233-BABY

www.evenflo.com

Residents of the United States can write to receive free promotional products from Evenflo. Residents of Canada can write to receive a free Evenflo product catalog.

This company has a multiple-birth program for twins, triplets, and quadruplets, available to residents of the United States and Canada. Write to receive free feeding items, including feeding bottles and a baby bib. You can register when the babies are born by sending a copy of the babies' birth certificates.

The First Years

In the United States or Canada, call 800-533-6708

www.thefirstyears.com

Call to receive a free product guide for parents. Visit the website to join the Parents Council to receive tips, parenting information, and free newsletters and to sign up for free contests and giveaways, as well as to have the opportunity to test and help develop new products. When you sign up to join the Parents Council, you can send free E-cards to friends and family members announcing the special first moments in your child's life.

This company has a multiple-birth program for parents of twins, triplets, quadruplets, or higher. To receive free bibs and rattles for each baby, register (after the babies are born) by sending copies of the babies' birth certificates, a newspaper announcement, or a hospital certificate to this address:

The First Years

Attn: Multiple Birth Program

One Kiddie Drive

Avon, MA 02322

These offers are available to residents of the United States and Canada.

❧ Flanders, Inc.
Marketing Services
P.O. Box 5323
Aiken, SC 29804
www.flandersbuttocksointment.com

For two free samples of Flanders Buttocks Ointment for diaper rash, send two loose first-class stamps with your name and address to Flanders. This offer is available to residents of the United States only.

❧ Food Stamp Program
See Chapter 7, "Free Government Resources for New or Expecting Parents," for information on how residents of the United States can receive free food stamps to buy nutritional foods for their family.

❧ Gerber Products Company (U.S.)
In the United States, call 800-4-GERBER
www.gerber.com/mygerber/register.asp

Call to receive coupons for baby food, a free informational booklet, and a free baby spoon. Check out Gerber's website to receive up to $50 (U.S.) in valuable coupons for Gerber products and more when you join Growing Up Gerber.

This company has a multiple-birth program for parents of twins, triplets, quadruplets, or higher. Please send copies of your babies' birth certificates to Gerber at the following address:

Gerber Products Company
Attn: Multiple Birth Program
445 State Street
Fremont, MI 49413

These offers are available to residents of the United States only.

❧ Gerber Products Company (Canada)

In Canada, call 800-4-GERBER

www.gerbercanada.com

Call to receive coupons for Gerber baby products, a free informational booklet, and a free baby spoon.

Please note: Gerber baby food is only available in the United States, but Gerber baby products, including breast-feeding products, baby care items, pacifiers, teethers, drinking cups, and more are sold in the United States, as well as in Canada.

This company has a multiple-birth program for parents of twins, triplets, quadruplets, or higher. Please send copies of your babies' birth certificates to Gerber at the following address:

Gerber Products Company
Attn: Multiple Birth Program
445 State Street
Fremont, MI 49413

These offers are available to residents of Canada only.

❧ Gymboree Play and Music

In the United States or Canada, call 800-520-PLAY

www.gymboree.com (click on "Play and Music Classes," then
　　"Attend a Free Class")

Gymboree offers play classes for children from newborn through 4 years of age and music classes for children 16 months through 4 years. Gymboree transforms colorful playscapes, creative activities, gentle sensory stimulation, and high-energy teachers into a fun-filled program for parents and children. Call to schedule a free preview class, or go online to print out a free class coupon. This offer is available to residents of the United States and Canada.

❧ Hain Celestial Group, Inc. (Earth's Best Baby Food)

In the United States or Canada, call 800-442-4221

www.earthsbest.com (click on "Promos")

Earth's Best is the only full line of organic baby food grown without potentially harmful pesticides, herbicides, or fertilizers. Call to register to receive a free brochure with money-saving coupons as well as for information on Earth's Best Baby Food. Residents of the United States can also register online to receive the Earth's Best newsletters with nutritional facts, environmental information, parenting tips, and special offers.

You can also register at the Earth's Best website to receive a free cereal bowl by sending in ten UPCs (universal product codes) from any Earth's Best products. Check the website for details.

(Earth's Best has partnered with Tushies. For further savings, look for the $1.50 [U.S.] off Earth's Best coupons on all Tushies packs.)

These offers are available to residents of the United States and Canada.

Healthtex
In the United States or Canada, call 800-554-7637
www.healthtex.com

Healthtex garments featuring Kidproof reduce shrinking, staining, and fading. To learn more about the wonders of Kidproof or to receive a free wallet-size child's immunization chart, call or visit the website. This offer is available to residents of the United States and Canada.

H. J. Heinz Company (Canada)
In Canada, call 800-565-2100
www.heinzbaby.com

Since 1991, Canadian parents have helped to raise more than $2 million (Canadian) for the Children's Miracle Network by sending in their Heinz baby labels! Call to participate in the Children's Miracle Network Program. This is a label-saving program where you can collect and send in the labels or box tops from any Heinz baby product. Through the Children's Miracle Network, Heinz will make a donation of 6¢ (for each label collected) to a local participating children's hospital. Call for further details. Start saving your labels today for a good cause!

Visit the Heinz website to get further information about the Heinz label-saving program, as well as to receive free Heinz Baby e-Flyers and other special offers from Heinz for new or expecting parents.

This company has a multiple-birth program for parents of twins, triplets, quadruplets, or higher. To receive free baby food and baby cereal, send copies of your babies' birth certificates to Heinz at the following address:

H. J. Heinz Company
Attn: Multiples
5700 Yonge Street
Suite 2100
North York, ON M2M 4K6

These offers are available to residents of Canada only.

H. J. Heinz Company (U.S.)
In the United States, call 800-USA-BABY

Call to receive a free feeding booklet with discount coupons, as well as other free promotional offers from Heinz.

This company has a multiple-birth program for parents of twins, triplets, quadruplets, or higher. Ask for details.

These offers are available to residents of the United States only.

Huggies
See Kimberly-Clark Corporation.

Invest in Kids
In Canada, call 877-583-KIDS
www.investinkids.ca

Invest in Kids is a not-for-profit foundation dedicated to the healthy social, emotional, and intellectual development of children from birth to age 5. Call or visit the website to receive a free Years Before Five Resource Kit, which discusses the importance of the early years and highlights the different development stages from birth to 5 years of age, as well as provides activities for each stage of your child's development. This offer is available to residents of Canada only.

❧ Johnson & Johnson (U.S.)

In the United States, call 800-526-3967
www.yourbaby.com/promo/NLSweepstakes/nls_pre_reg.asp

Parents can call to receive a free baby care basics brochure with valuable coupons, as well as to receive occasional mailings with further offers from Johnson & Johnson.

Visit the BabyCenter website (www.babycenter.com) to sign up for a free personalized newsletter. When you sign up, you will automatically be entered for a chance to win a diaper bag filled with $50 worth of Johnson's Baby products. There is one winner each month.

This company has a multiple-birth program for parents of twins, triplets, quadruplets, or higher. Ask for details.

These offers are available to residents of the United States only.

❧ Johnson & Johnson (Canada)

In Canada, call 800-361-8068
www.jnjcanada.com

Call Johnson & Johnson to receive a New Parent's Pack with free samples, coupons, and literature. This offer is available to residents of Canada only.

❧ Kimberly-Clark Corporation (Huggies)

In the United States or Canada, call 800-544-1847
www.huggies.com/diaperswipes/specialoffers

Huggies offers a free Rewards Program. When you purchase various Huggies products, you will receive points toward items from the Rewards Program brochure. Simply save and cut out the proof-of-purchase labels on Huggies products. You will receive Huggies

Rewards points each time you purchase one of the following: Huggies Diapers, Huggies Pull-Ups, Huggies Baby Wipes, or Huggies Little Swimmers.

Call to receive a free Rewards Program brochure and you will also get a postcard to be added to Huggies' mailing list for new or expecting parents. You will receive coupons for Huggies Diapers, Baby Wipes, and other promotional items and free samples that are being offered at the time. Huggies will also send out occasional mailings and coupons at the different stages of your baby's development.

You can also register online to join the Huggies Special Offers mailing list to receive money-saving coupons, a quarterly E-mail subscription to *The Happy Baby Times*, and more. Visit the website for details.

This company has a multiple-birth program for parents of twins, triplets, quadruplets, or higher. To receive a one-time gift of coupons, send copies of your babies' birth certificates to:

Kimberly-Clark Corporation
Department QMB
P.O. Box 2020
Neenah, WI 54957-2020

or:

Kimberly-Clark, Inc.
Department QMB
50 Burnhamthorpe Road West
Mississauga, ON L5B 3Y5

These offers are available to residents of the United States and Canada.

Kushies

336 Green Road
Stoney Creek, ON L8E 2B2
In the United States or Canada, call 800-841-5330
www.kooshies.com

Kushies has a multiple-birth program for parents of twins, triplets, quadruplets, or higher, from newborn to 3 months of age. To receive free gifts for your babies, send Kushies copies of your babies' birth certificates or a letter from the hospital where you gave birth, together with the names and genders of your babies. This offer is available to residents of the United States and Canada.

Lansinoh Laboratories, Inc.
In the United States or Canada, call 800-292-4794

Call to receive a free sample of their soothing and protecting breast-feeding cream made with pure lanolin. This offer is available to residents of the United States and Canada.

Little Remedies Products
In the United States, call 800-754-8853
www.littleremedies.com

"We Make It All Better," claims Little Remedies Products, by providing safe, gentle relief of the common discomforts experienced by infants and children, without the addition of harmful preservatives or unnecessary additives. To receive valuable coupons and information from Little Remedies, call or go online to view the complete product line and special offers. This offer is available to residents of the United States only.

Little Tykes
In the United States or Canada, call 800-321-0183

Call Little Tykes to be added to their mailing list to receive free promotional items and a Little Tykes catalog. This offer is available to residents of the United States and Canada.

Materna New Moms Club
See Wyeth-Ayerst Canada Inc.

❧ McNeil Consumer Healthcare

In the United States, call 800-962-5357

In Canada, call 800-265-7323

www.mcneilcanada.com

Call to receive coupons for Infants' or Children's Tylenol or for Children's Motrin, a medical recording booklet for your child, or free promotional offers from Johnson & Johnson. This offer is available to residents of the United States and Canada.

In Canada, call 888-6-MOTRIN to receive coupons for Children's Motrin and a free copy of the booklet *Ask a Paediatrician*. In this booklet, a panel of pediatricians and family doctors answer the questions parents ask most often about safely treating a child's pain and fever. This offer is available to residents of Canada only.

❧ Mead Johnson Nutritionals (U.S.)

In the United States, call 800-BABY-123

www.meadjohnson.com (click on "Nutrition for You," then
   "Enfamil Family of Formulas")

Call or register online to take part in the free Enfamil Family Beginnings Program and receive valuable retail checks and special offers.

Visit www.enfamil.com/enfamil8.html and print out the page to pack in your suitcase and give to your nurse at the hospital when your baby arrives to receive a free diaper bag and other free samples, educational materials, critical safety information, and a hearing health checklist, compliments of the Enfamil Family of Formulas. (This offer is available at participating hospitals.)

This company has a multiple-birth program for parents of twins, triplets, quadruplets, or higher. Ask for details.

These offers are available to residents of the United States only.

❧ Mead Johnson Nutritionals (Canada)

In Canada, call 800-361-6323

www.enfalac.ca

Residents of Canada can call to receive discounts on baby formula and to join the Enfalac Baby Steps Program. When you join Enfalac Baby Steps, here's what you will receive:

1. A keepsake box with a free product sample and coupons, along with informational brochures.
2. Three booklets to help you make informed decisions about the best nutritional care for the growth and development of you and your baby. Each booklet comes with quick and easy reference cards to hang on your fridge. These reference cards can also be used as flash cards to entertain and stimulate your baby; they contain information on subjects like the stages of labor, ways to soothe your crying baby, and more.
3. A free nutritional information book titled *Nourishing Your Baby*. You can also register online to join Baby Steps.

This company has a multiple-birth program for parents of twins, triplets, quadruplets, or higher. Ask for details.

These offers are available to residents of Canada only.

Milupa
2300 Monterey Road
Laval, QC H7L 3H9
In Canada, call 866-335-9080

Call or write to Milupa to receive a free baby spoon, a "Baby in Car" bumper sticker, a discount coupon for money off Milupa infant cereal, as well as a free nutrition guide. This offer is available to residents of Canada only.

Mommies Choice
c/o Tammy Brannigan
490 Third Street
Unit 12
London, ON N5V 4A2
www.mommieschoice.com

To receive a free sample of Mommies Best Powder (with no added zinc, talc, fragrance, preservatives, or dyes, an all-natural solution to diaper rash), send a self-addressed, stamped envelope with one first-class stamp for residents of Canada and two first-class stamps for residents of the United States. You can also send an E-mail request to tammy brannigan@mommieschoice.com. This offer is available to residents of the United States and Canada.

❧ The Mom Pack
See Preciouskids.org.

❧ Mother's Little Miracle
1815 Via El Prado
Suite 400
Redondo Beach, CA 90277
In the United States or Canada, call 310-540-3727 (sorry, not a toll-
   free number)

Parents of triplets or more can call or write to receive a free three-item gift box of baby cleaning products from Mother's Little Miracle. Send copies of your babies' birth certificates. This offer is available to residents of the United States and Canada.

❧ National Institute of Child Health and Human Development
In the United States, call 800-370-2943
www.nichd.nih.gov (click on "Back to Sleep")

The Back to Sleep Campaign is a program that provides information on SIDS (sudden infant death syndrome) and the importance of placing healthy babies on their backs to sleep. Residents of the United States can call to receive free SIDS safety stickers, a magnet, a door hanger reminding you to put your baby to sleep on his or her back, and a brochure that offers information about SIDS and how to protect your infant. Residents of the United States or Canada can order online.

❦ Nature's One

In the United States, call 614-898-9758

www.naturesone.com

Baby's Only Organic pediatric infant formula is made with organic ingredients. Call for a free sample of either the dairy-based or soy-based infant formula.

For every twenty-four proof-of-purchase seals that you collect and save from Nature's One products, you will be sent a coupon for two free units of the same product. Click on "Product Rebate" at the website for instructions on how you can receive a free mail-in rebate. You also have the option of pledging your free product to Feed the Children. Check the Feed the Children website (www.feedthechildren.org) for details. Nature's One will donate a portion of its after-tax profits in the form of money and product to help support Feed the Children.

These offers are available to residents of the United States only.

❦ Nestlé Carnation Infant Nutrition (Canada)

In Canada, call 800-387-5536

www.nestle.ca/english

Call the above-listed number to receive a FREE subscription to the *Nestlé Good Start Magazine* for expecting and new moms. The magazine provides information, advice, and support for you and your growing baby—from nutrition tips to parenting insights and everything in between. Along with your free magazine subscription, you will receive valuable coupons, free samples of infant formula and baby cereal (if you choose), plus information and savings on special products for new parents. You can also subscribe online to the *Good Start Magazine* by visiting the website listed above.

This company also has a multiple-birth program where parents of multiples will receive a free case of the infant formula of their choice, including Good Start or Alsoy infant formula.

Register as soon as you are expecting to receive the greatest benefits from this program. Please call the toll-free number for details on how to register. These offers are available to residents of Canada only.

❦ Nestlé Carnation Infant Nutrition (U.S.)
In the United States, call 800-242-5200
www.verybestbaby.com

Call to join the Very Best Baby to receive a free six-month subscription to Carnation's *The Very Best Baby* magazine, as well as to receive free money-saving checks for Carnation Infant Nutrition products.

You can also register online to join the Very Best Baby. When you register online to join, you can choose to receive an assortment of free benefits, including *The Very Best Baby* magazine, checks for savings on infant nutrition products, periodic E-mail updates, special notices for promotional offers, products and services, personalized website content that is specifically designed for your stage of pregnancy or the age of your baby, an interactive chart that allows you to track your weight gain during your pregnancy, tools to help you chart your baby's growth, and more.

This company also has a multiple-birth program where parents of twins, triples, quadruplets, or higher can receive free cans of infant formula, a free subscription to *The Very Best Baby* magazine, and money-saving checks for infant nutrition products. Copies of your babies' birth certificates are required. Call for details on how you can sign up for this program.

These offers are available to residents of the United States only.

❦ Novartis Consumer Health (Triaminic)
In the United States, call 888-935-5543

Call to join the Triaminic New Parents' Club and receive the *Triaminic Parents' Club* magazine, savings coupons, and more. This offer is available to residents of the United States only.

❦ Ocean Spray Cranberries, Inc.
Customer Service
One Ocean Spray Drive
Lakeville-Middleboro, MA 02349
In the United States or Canada, call 800-662-3263
www.oceanspray.com

Call or write to request Ocean Spray's free booklet titled *What's This Stuff?! A Parent's Guide to Coping with Picky Eaters.* You will also be sent a recipe booklet and product coupons and gift certificates for free Ocean Spray products. Include a copy of your baby's birth certificate with your written request to Ocean Spray. This offer is available to residents of the United States and Canada.

❀ Our Kids, Inc.

www.baby-be-safe.com
In the United States, call 877-909-7684
In Canada, call 561-741-3344 (sorry, not a toll-free number)

Our Kids offers 100 percent cotton crib sheets that stay secure to crib mattresses and are easy for an adult to change. In addition to a flat secure crib sheet, Our Kids offers Baby-Be-Safe crib sheets that come with an elevation wedge. They are the only sheets on the market today that come with an elevation sleep wedge that stays securely in place. These sheets are recommended by pediatricians for their safety and medical benefits. When you call to order a free brochure, you will also be sent a free emergency wipe board, as well as fabric samples for Baby-Be-Safe crib sheets. This offer is available to residents of the United States only.

❀ Pampers

See Procter & Gamble.

❀ ParentPak

A Division of Creative Expressions
PMB 158
3509 Baker Road
Suite 403
Acworth, GA 30101
www.parentpak.com

The ParentPak is a free informational gift pack (from Creative Expressions and the Parent Resource Group) for expectant or new parents. This pack contains a resource guide with childbirth, breast-feeding, and parenting information, as well as product information, coupons, samples, and more. As this package weighs a good 2 pounds, a shipping fee of $4.50 (U.S.) is charged to cover the cost of shipping the pack to U.S. addresses and $7.50 (U.S.) to ship to Canadian addresses. Send a check or money order to Creative Expressions at the address above. (Please write "Free Stuff for Baby!" on the front of the envelope.) You may also order online using your credit card. This offer is available to residents of the United States and Canada.

❦ PBM Products, Inc. (America's Store Brand Infant Formulas)
In the United States, call 800-485-9969
www.storebrandformulas.com

Call to receive a free sample of Babymil, Babysoy, Parent's Choice, or other store-brand infant formula. This offer is available to residents of the United States only. Limit one per household.

❦ Pharmascience
In Canada, call 888-550-6060
www.pharmascience.com

Pharmascience are the makers of Pediatric Electrolyte, which helps to prevent dehydration in children and infants with diarrhea; Rhinaris Pediatric Drops and Gel for dry nose discomfort; Rhinaris Pediatric Saline Solution; and other infant and children's medical products. For information about their products, and to receive discount coupons and/or free product samples, please call the Pharmascience Medical Information Hotline number listed above. This offer is available to residents of Canada only.

❦ Playtex Products, Inc.
In Canada, call 800-387-1300
www.playtexbaby.com
www.playtexproductsinc.com

Call Playtex to join the Joy of Feeding Program and receive a free informational brochure, Playtex product coupons, and more.

This company has a multiple-birth program for parents of twins, triplets, quadruplets, or higher. Ask for details.

These offers are available to residents of Canada only.

❦ **Playtex Products, Inc. (Diaper Genie)**
   20 Troy Road
   Whippany, NJ 07981
   In the United States or Canada, call 800-843-6430
   www.playtexbaby.com

Parents of multiples can call or write to receive free Diaper Genie rebate certificates. Send your name, your mailing address, and copies of your babies' birth certificates or birth announcements. (Your request must be sent before your babies turn 3 months of age.) This offer is available to residents of the United States and Canada.

❦ **Polly Klaas Foundation**
   In the United States or Canada, call 800-587-4357
   www.pollyklaas.org (click on "Child Safety Kit")

The Polly Klaas Foundation, which aids in the search for missing children, is dedicated to educating parents on protecting their children from child abduction, as well as other safety issues. Call for a free Child Safety Kit with fingerprint and DNA capabilities. There is no fee for the ID kits; however, a donation of $3 is appreciated to help cover shipping and handling costs. You can register to receive one kit for each child in your family. This free kit includes the following:

- *Polly Klaas Foundation History and Activities*
- *Your Child . . . the Truth*
- *Child Identification Booklet*
- *Child Safety: Important Information You Should Know*
- *Parental Abductions . . . the Truth*
- *Runaways . . . the Truth*
- *Internet Abduction . . . the Truth*

Safety kits cost the foundation approximately 76¢ to produce and 78¢ (U.S.) to mail. While the foundation continues to take requests, please be aware that it receives no government funding and the organization exists strictly because of donations. This offer is available to residents of the United States and Canada.

✿ Preciouskids.org

P.O. Box 271

Banks, OR 97106

www.preciouskids.org/mompack.html

Order your free Mom Pack filled with flyers, coupons, and samples from several moms with home-based businesses. The pack is absolutely free, but because of the size and weight of the pack, you should send either six postage stamps if you reside in the United States, $2 in postage if you live in Canada, or $2 (U.S.) to cover the cost of shipping. You can also order your free Mom Pack online. This offer is available to residents of the United States and Canada.

✿ Procter & Gamble (Pampers)

In the United States or Canada, call 800-543-0480

or 800-726-7377

www.pampers.com (click on "Join Pampers.com")

Call to be put on the company mailing list to receive sample products and disposable diaper coupons. Call again after your baby is born to receive further offers. Pampers will also send out occasional mailings and coupons at the different stages of your baby's development.

When you register online, you will receive a free newsletter, a $10 New Registration Coupon Book, private product previews and samples from Pampers, as well as special offers from other Procter & Gamble brands. This offer is available to residents of the United States and Canada.

This company has a multiple-birth program for parents of twins, triplets, quadruplets, or higher. To receive a free, one-time gift offer from Pampers, mail your name and address, along with copies of your babies' birth certificates (or verification of birth on your doctor's letterhead stationery), to:

Pampers Multiple Birth Offer
The Procter & Gamble Company
P.O. Box 599
Cincinnati, OH 45201

or:

Pampers Multiple Birth Offer
The Procter & Gamble Company
P.O. Box 355, Station A
Toronto, ON M5W 1C5

❧ Ringling Bros. and Barnum & Bailey Circus
Baby Program
Feld Entertainment, Inc.
Attn: Customer Relations
8607 Westwood Center Drive
Vienna, VA 22182
www.ringling.com/offers

If you love the circus, here's something you won't want to miss! The Ringling Bros. and Barnum & Bailey Circus is giving every child born during the past twelve months his or her first ticket to "The Greatest Show on Earth" absolutely free! Write for one free ticket per child, or fill out the online form to request your free ticket. In your written request, please include your name, your home address and phone number, your child's first name and birth date, together with a photocopy of your child's birth certificate. (Tickets are good for an unlimited time.) This offer is available to residents of the United States only.

Parents of multiples can request free tickets by mailing copies of their babies' birth certificates to Ringling Bros. and Barnum & Bailey Circus.

❦ Sassy, Inc.

In the United States or Canada, call 800-323-6336
www.sassybaby.com

Sassy offers educational and stimulating products for your baby. Call to receive a free product brochure, as well as a free copy of Sassy's sleep brochure *Sweet Dreams for Baby and You: A Guide to Helping Baby Establish Healthy Sleep Habits.*

Sassy's product brochure contains four "Buy 1, Get 1 Free" offers for parents of twins, triplets, quadruplets, or higher. When parents of multiples buy one of these four infant products listed in the brochure, they will be sent an identical item, free of charge.

These offers are available to residents of the United States and Canada.

Residents of the United States can also register online to join Sassy's free Parent's Club.

❦ Similac Welcome Addition Club (U.S.)

In the United States, call 800-BABYLINE
www.welcomeaddition.com (click on "Join the Club")

Call or go online to join the Similac Welcome Addition Club. Member benefits may include money-saving discounts, free samples of Similac Infant Formulas, periodic newsletters containing expert pregnancy and parenting advice, or other gifts. This offer is available to residents of the United States only.

❦ Similac Welcome Addition Club (Canada)

P.O. Box 130
Station Pointe Claire
Pointe Claire, QC H9R 9Z9
In Canada, call 800-518-CLUB

Call or write to join the Welcome Addition Club to receive coupons and free samples of Similac and other infant formulas, as well as a free gift or sample kit for your baby. This company will also send you occasional mailings with information on your baby's growth and development. This offer is available to residents of Canada only.

❦ Snow Pharmaceuticals, LLC (Snow Balm)
P.O. Box 29
Selbyville, DE 19975
www.snowbalm.com/sampleı.htm

For a free sample of Snow Balm diaper rash ointment, send two first-class stamps to Snow Pharmaceuticals. Also send your name, address, E-mail address, and phone number, as well as the birth dates of children still in diapers. When sending for your sample, please mention that you saw our listing in *Free Stuff for Baby!* Be sure to print your information. This offer is available for a limited time and is only available to residents of the United States. (To be sure of the availability of the current offer, visit the website.)

❦ State of Virginia (Child Safety Seat Program)
In the United States, call 800-732-8333
www.safetyseatva.org/lowincome.htm

Through its Child Safety Seat Program, the Virginia Department of Health provides free child safety seats to qualifying low-income families in the state of Virginia. More than seven thousand seats are provided each year with funding from the Child Restraint Special Device Fund and are distributed through local health departments.

To qualify for a free child safety seat, applicants must be legal residents of Virginia; must be eligible for Medicaid; must be a parent, legal guardian, or foster parent of the child; and must be, at the earliest, in the last trimester of pregnancy. Recipients are also required to attend a safety seat installation and use class. Check out the website or call for further information and details on how you can receive a free child safety seat.

For those residing outside the state of Virginia, some hospitals and health departments provide new moms with free infant car seats upon giving birth to their new baby at the hospital. Call the hospital where you will be giving birth to see if they have a similar program available to expecting moms.

✿ Stork's Choice Disposable Diaper Service
In the United States, call 877-67-STORK
www.storkschoice.com/sample.asp (click on "Order Sample Pack")

Stork's Choice offers a free sample package containing eight Stork's Choice premium disposable diapers or four Stork's Choice premium training pants. There is no charge for the samples, but there is a shipping and handling fee of $2.99. To receive a sample package, fill out the online form or call. This offer is available to residents of the United States only.

✿ Transport Canada
In the United States or Canada, call 800-333-0371
www.tc.gc.ca/roadsafety (click on "Child Safety")

Transport Canada offers a free video, "Car Time 1-2-3-4," and its companion booklet, *Keep Kids Safe*, to help parents properly use and install a child seat in a motor vehicle. The video shows how and when to use rear-facing infant seats, forward-facing child seats, booster seats, and seat belts. An information guide on how to install and use child restraint systems is included in this package. You can request the free video and booklet by calling or visiting the website and filling out a request form. You can also call Transport Canada for more information on child car seat safety. This offer is available to residents of the United States and Canada.

✿ Triaminic
See Novartis Consumer Health.

❧ Tushies

In the United States, call 800-344-6379
www.tushies.com

Tushies offers a wide assortment of diapers and baby products online. Call to request a free Tushies diaper sample. Tushies is also offering a free Tushies.com tote bag with your first Tushies or Tendercare Club order. Check out the website or call for further details. (This offer is available for a limited time only.) Tushies has a free diaper club where you will receive better prices on Tushies baby products and convenient, automatic delivery every three to six weeks. Call or check the website for details.

These offers are available to residents of the United States only.

❧ Welcome Wagon

In Canada, call 800-301-1104
www.welcomewagon.ca/en/baby/home_baby.html

Welcome Wagon is a Canadian-owned free greeting service. If you are a new or expecting mom, Welcome Wagon will greet you with a friendly visit, providing you with free coupons, brochures, and gifts for your baby, as well as a complimentary copy of *Baby Stages* magazine. You can call Welcome Wagon at the toll-free number listed above or call the nearest Welcome Wagon to have a representative contact you. (Welcome Wagon is listed in the white pages in your local telephone book.) You can also fill out Welcome Wagon's online request form to have a representative contact you. In order to receive your free gifts from Welcome Wagon, you must be expecting or have a newborn. This offer is available to residents of Canada only.

❧ Welcome Wagon Baby Shower

In Canada, call 800-301-1104
www.welcomewagon.ca/en/baby/signup/signup_baby.html
www.welcomewagon.ca/en (click on "Upcoming Shows")

A Welcome Wagon Baby Shower is a free group function for expecting moms that is held at various locations throughout Canada. This fun and educational baby shower provides educational speakers, displays, shows, and more for the expecting mom. To register, call to receive a free invitation to a Welcome Wagon Baby Shower for expectant mothers. You can also fill out an online form to request a baby shower. To find out when a Welcome Wagon Baby Shower will be held in your area, visit the website to view the various locations, dates, and times. This offer is available to residents of Canada only.

❦ Weleda Newborn Kit
In the United States, call 800-241-1030

Weleda offers free product samples off and on throughout the year. Call for information on current offers. You can also call to receive a free Weleda catalog featuring quality baby care and personal care products. This offer is available to residents of the United States only.

❦ White House
Greetings Office
1600 Pennsylvania Avenue NW
Washington, DC 20500

The president of the United States would like to welcome your newest arrival to the world with a special signed congratulatory announcement. Simply send a copy of your baby's birth announcement or write a note with your baby's date of birth to the White House.

❦ WIC (Women, Infants, and Children)
See Chapter 7, "Free Government Resources for New or Expecting Parents," to find out how low-income families in the United States can receive—free from the government—nutritious foods, infant formula, and cereal during their baby's first years.

❦ Window Covering Safety Council

In the United States or Canada, call 800-506-4636

www.windowcoverings.org (click on "Free Cord Safety Kits")

There have been a number of incidents where children have strangled in the loops of window blind and curtain cords. Be sure that your blinds do not have looped cords. To assist in this safety precaution, the Window Covering Safety Council offers free childproofing kits to help prevent cord accidents related to window blinds. The organization will provide free safety tassels, cord stops, and tie-down devices, as well as instructions on how to install these safety devices. Call for details. This offer is available to residents of the United States and Canada.

❦ Wyeth-Ayerst Canada Inc. (Materna New Moms Club)

P.O. Box 397

Stn. Port Credit

Mississauga, ON L5G 9Z9

In Canada, call 888-597-8016

When you join, Materna will send you free birth announcement cards, samples, and valuable product coupons. Call for details on how to join, or send a written request with your name, address, phone number, and due date. This offer is available to residents of Canada only.

❦ Wyeth Consumer Healthcare

5 Giralda Farms

Madison, NJ 07940

In the United States or Canada, call 888-797-5638

Call or write to be placed on Wyeth's mailing list to receive free coupons for money off Wyeth products, including Children's Advil, Dimetapp, and Anbesol. This offer is available to residents of the United States and Canada.

This company has a multiple-birth program offering free product coupons for Wyeth products to parents of twins, triplets, quadruplets, or higher. Ask for details.

❦ Xttrium Laboratories

415 West Pershing Road
Chicago, IL 60609
In the United States or Canada, call 800-587-3721
www.xttrium.com

Call to receive free trial-size samples of DRC, a fragrance-free and water-repellant diaper rash cream, together with a mail-in rebate coupon. This offer is available to residents of the United States and Canada.

Baby Freebies on the Net

Cyber freak, cyber geek—call me what you like, but I just can't seem to get enough of the Internet. With a few clicks of the mouse, you can chat with other parents from around the world, get up-to-date on the latest baby products, swap baby food recipes, and read about other parents' birth experiences. Literally anything and everything to do with babies and parenting can be found on the World Wide Web.

There are hundreds, if not thousands, of baby websites on the Internet, and I have been to many of them, surfing the Net until the wee hours of the morning to find the best online deals for you and your baby.

So for all of you computer-savvy parents out there, here is a listing of some great websites that offer even more terrific freebies.

If you don't own a computer, maybe you can borrow one from a friend or get online at your local library. Most libraries now have computers that you can use free of charge. There are some great online offers here that you won't want to miss.

❀ Amphion Communications
www.2bparent.com/calen3dar.htm

This website offers a free fetal development calendar where you can find out when your baby will acquire new abilities. This offer is available to residents of the United States only.

❧ Anbesol

www.anbesol.com/teething/chart.asp

Visit the Anbesol website to receive a free printable baby tooth chart to keep track of when each of your baby's first teeth appear.

❧ Babies Online Automated Birth Announcement System

www.babiesonline.com

Show off your new bundle of joy to friends and family around the world with Babies Online automated birth announcement system. Your baby can have her own Web page, complete with pictures, music, your choice of background style, and your own guest book. It only takes a few minutes to create—and it's free!

❧ Babies Online Pregnancy Planner

www.babiesonline.com/pregnancy/planner/content.asp

Babies Online offers a free pregnancy planner that calculates the preferred days for getting pregnant. If you are planning for a girl or a boy, the planner also suggests some actions that may influence the sex of the child, based on scientific research.

❧ Baby BumbleBee

www.babybumblebee.com/v2/pages/freebies.cfm

Baby BumbleBee provides parents with educationally appropriate materials, including educational videos and more, for infants and toddlers. The website offers an assortment of valuable teaching tools for your baby that you can print out for free. Alphabet Posters are colorful posters that can be printed out and placed around your baby's room to help teach the alphabet. Number Posters are colorful posters that you can print out and place around your baby's room to help teach number recognition and counting. Bee Smart Baby Vocabulary Builder Flashcards can be used to enhance your infant's language acquisition. The Infant Safety Checklist will provide you with information for making your home safe for your baby. Some of the topics include kitchen and bathroom safety, choking, poisoning, hazardous items, electrical hazards, and car and crib safety. Parents of infants and toddlers will want to read the page called "Tips for Promoting Speech and Language Development," with great tips and ideas to help develop your baby's speech and language.

❧ BabyCenter
www.babycenter.com

The BabyCenter website offers a free membership where you will receive weekly development updates, as well as free online birth announcements. This website also includes an easy-to-follow milestone chart, advice on when to call the doctor, chat rooms, an immunization scheduler, and more.

❧ Baby Food Recipes
www.nncc.org (click on "Information Station," then "Infant and
    Toddler Care," then "Nutrition")

This National Network for Child Care website offers information on nutrition, feeding your baby, and recipes to make your own nutritious baby food.

❧ Baby Orajel
www.orajel.com/rebate.html

Visit the website to find out how you can receive a manufacturer's mail-in refund on the purchase of any Orajel or Baby Orajel product for toothache, teething, or oral care needs. This offer is available to residents of the United States only.

❧ BabyPlans
www.babyplans.com/newadditionsmenu.html

At BabyPlans you can announce the birth of your new bundle of joy by creating a free home page for the world to see!

❦ BabyZone

www.babyzone.com (click on "Free Stuff")

Register online to receive free stuff, including coupons and catalogs for new or expecting parents. Just for fun, try to predict the sex of your baby by using this free online Chinese lunar calendar (www.babyzone.com/babynames/chinese.asp). It is believed that this chart has been proven by thousands of people and is 99 percent accurate!

❦ Born to Love

www.borntolove.com/catalogues.html (click on "Choose Your Free
      Newsletters")

The Born to Love website offers an assortment of baby newsletters that you can receive free via E-mail, including *Baby Marketplace*, *This Baby of Mine*, *Parentsline News*, and more. This offer is available to residents of the United States only.

❦ Brighter Vision Learning Adventures

www.brightervision.com (click on "Free Offer")

Brighter Vision offers a variety of early childhood educational material for children ages 1 to 6. Fill out Brighter Vision's online reply form to get a free shipment of fun-filled educational materials for your child. Each Learning Adventure shipment contains an activity book, a hardcover storybook, a hands-on project, a parent's newsletter, fun stickers, and more. No purchase is necessary, and you may cancel at any time or return any shipment you don't want. The first shipment is free and yours to keep in any case. Log on to Brighter Vision's website for more information. This offer is available to residents of the United States only.

❧ Bryce Foster Corporation (Fresh Sacks)
www.freshsacks.com

Fresh Sacks are convenient diaper disposal bags that are designed to eliminate diaper odor. Visit their website to receive a free five-bag sample pack and a manufacturer's rebate. Fresh Sacks are available at Walgreens nationwide. This offer is available to residents of the United States only.

❧ Canadian Parents Online Baby Food Recipes
www.canadianparents.com/canadacooks (click on "Baby Food")

This website contains some great, nutritious baby food recipes that you can make at home in your food processor or blender.

❧ Charmin
www.charmin.com/en_us/pages/pt.shtml

Visit the website to sign up to receive a free potty-training kit. This fun and adorable potty-training kit will help you teach your child proper bathroom habits. Each kit includes a free "Ready . . . Set . . . Go!" poster to hang up in your bathroom as a reminder for your little one, stickers to match to each of the steps in the poster, a cute storybook, a picture frame magnet, and a roll ruler. The Charmin roll ruler hangs on the toilet roll to teach kids exactly how much tissue to use. Once your child has successfully completed potty training, you can recognize his or her achievement with a diploma from "Charmin University." This offer is available to residents of the United States and Canada.

❧ Chart Jungle
www.chartjungle.com/pottycharts.html

Chart Jungle offers free potty time charts and certificates for completing potty training for boys and girls. You can use stickers or markers on these adorable potty charts to mark off the days of the week.

There are an assortment of other free charts that you can print out at Chart Jungle as well, including bedtime charts with bedtime reminders, free award charts, "Mom, I'm Bored" charts with activity suggestions, chore charts, and more.

 Childavenue

www.childavenue.com (click on "Family Corner")

This parenting website offers a free printable Potty Training Reward chart for your child.

 Computer Mommy

www.computermommy.com/computerbaby/index.html (click on "Computer Baby")

This website offers a free printable faces page for your baby.

Cosco

www.coscoinc.com/services/rebate/juvrebt.htm

From time to time, the Cosco Rebate website offers an assortment of mail-in rebates on baby products, including the Diaper Nanny, infant car seats, booster seats, toddler beds, high chairs, strollers, baby exercisers, and more. This offer is available to residents of the United States only.

David Jack

www.davidjack.com/freetape.html

To introduce you to the quality children's music of David Jack, this website offers, free of charge, the children's music CD titled *Dance in Your Pants*. You pay only the shipping and handling. Check out the website for further details.

December Fifth Creations Baby Shower Games

www.dfcreations.com/BabyShower.html

At this website you'll find more than fifty humorous, creative, challenging, and ice-breaking baby shower games! This assortment of free games includes "My Water Broke," "Pin the Diaper on the Baby," "Taste Test Baby Food Game," "Mom-to-Be Trivia Game," "Guess the Delivery Stats," "Diaper Bag Mystery," and more.

✿ Dimetapp (Wyeth Consumer Healthcare)
www.dimetapp.com

Visit Dimetapp's website to receive a free coupon for money off Dimetapp Infant Drops. This offer is available to residents of the United States only.

✿ Drypers Goodie Pack (Associated Hygienic Products)
www.drypers.com/goodie.asp

Sign up online to receive Drypers' free pack of goodies for new parents, which includes the *Smart Mom's Little Book of Tricks*, a guide with ideas for stress relief, valuable coupons, and more.

When you receive your free Goodie Pack, you'll also find a special form enclosed that you can fill out for your baby's grandparents to receive a subscription to *The Grand Life*, a quarterly electronic newsletter, with E-mail notification of special offers and more. Grandparents can also sign up to join the Drypers Grandparents Club at www.drypers.com. This offer is available to residents of the United States and Canada.

At www.drypers.com/shower.html you will find an assortment of terrific ideas for throwing a baby shower, including games and other fun stuff.

✿ Early Pregnancy Test Kit
www.iparenting.com/ept (click on "Coupon")

Visit the website to receive a free online coupon for money off e.p.t., a one-step home pregnancy test from Pfizer Inc.

❧ Enfamil

www.efb-mail.com/home.html

The Enfamil website offers free online cards that you can send to a friend or relative. These cute cards contain a section where you can add your own personal message. Themes for these cards include "Pregnancy," "It's A Girl!," "It's A Boy!," "Congratulations," "Birthday," "Thank You," and "Grandparents." Some of these cards are even animated!

❧ Envisage Design Oh Baby!

www.envisagedesign.com/ohbaby

Researchers have found that babies prefer to look at high-contrast images. The Envisage Design website provides free infant stimulation graphics that you can download and print out for your baby to help increase your baby's concentration skills as well as attention span.

❧ First Response

www.1stresponse.com/brochures/coupon.asp

Log on to the First Response website to receive a coupon booklet with up to $60 in savings for you and your baby. This free coupon booklet contains valuable discount coupons on First Response Ovulation and Pregnancy Test Kits, as well as savings from Cosco, Tums, and more. This offer is available to residents of the United States only.

❧ Fisher-Price Family

www.fisher-price.com/us/family/form.asp

Residents of the United States can join the Fisher-Price Family mailing list to receive special offers from Fisher-Price, contests, age-appropriate updates for your child, free E-mail and newsletters, news on latest products, and more.

❧ Fisher-Price Little People Club

www.fisherprice.com/us/littlepeople/birthday/default.asp

To help your little one celebrate his very first birthday, join the Little People Club to receive a free Little People 1st Birthday Kit, complete with party invitations, valuable coupons for money off Little People toys, *Parents' Guide to Planning the Biggest Little 1st Birthday Party Ever*, and more. The club is free to join, but be sure to join well in advance of your child's first birthday as it may take up to six weeks to receive the kit.

The Little People Club has even more surprises in store for your child! Soon after you receive your birthday kit in the mail, you'll also get a free Little People "Discovering Animals" video.

Garanimals

www.garanimals.com/contact_us.asp

Register online for a free growth chart for your child. This offer is available to residents of the United States only.

GoodNites (Kimberly-Clark)

www.goodnites.com/sample

Register online to receive a free printable coupon for money off your next purchase of GoodNites disposable underpants. This offer is available to residents of the United States only.

Growing Family

www.growingfamily.com

Growing Family is a company dedicated to helping families and is the leading, in-hospital infant photo service provider in the United States and Canada. Growing Family offers new parents free membership in the Growing Family Network. As your baby grows from infant to toddler, you will receive new offers to meet your child's new needs from Growing Family and a select group of leading companies. Visit the website to register for your free membership. This offer is available to residents of the United States and Canada.

❦ GrowthSpurts.com
www.growthspurts.com

At GrowthSpurts.com you can create a free website for your child where you can upload your child's photos to share with your family and friends, as well as track your child's growth and development.

❦ Heinz Baby Basics
www.vitalbaby.com/basics/offer.html

Join the Heinz Baby Basics mailing list to receive a free baby spoon from the Heinz Baby Basics line, as well as details on future offers and specials, by filling out the form at the website. This offer is available to residents of Canada only.

❦ Huggies Happy Baby Fun
www.huggies.com/happybabyfun/hppybby.asp

At this cute and creative website you can make and print out a personalized storybook for your child. Your child will love it when she hears her own name in the story! This website also offers a personalized coloring book for your child to make and print out, plus customized picture frames, a Happy Baby Growth Chart, Create-a-Mobile, songs, games, and more.

❦ Huggies Super Sweepstakes
www.huggies.com/sweepstakes/index.asp

Fill out the online entry form to win a year's supply of Huggies Diapers and Huggies Baby Wipes. This offer is available to residents of the United States and Canada.

❦ Hyland's
www.hylands.com (click on "Consumer Promotions")

Off and on, Hyland's offers promotions and discounts on diaper rash cream, children's medicines, and various other products at the website. If a free promotional offer is not available the first time you visit the website, check back again at a later time.

✺ KidKits
www.whatsshowing.on.ca/kids

Free child ID kits are available at this website. In the event your child goes missing, this printable KidKit will provide police with vital information about him or her.

✺ KIDSAFE ID
www.kidsafeid.com

This terrific child safety website allows you to customize, create, and print out your own free KIDSAFE ID Card for your child. Parents can choose from more than thirty colorful, kid-friendly backgrounds, including baby boy, baby girl, dress-up, baseball, ballet, music, and more. Visit the website for further details. And while you're there, click on "Do-It-Yourself DNA Kit" to learn how to prepare a home sample of DNA material for your child. All that is required is a cotton swab and two resealable bags. It's really simple to make and worth the effort!

✺ KidsNfeet
www.kidsnshoes.com/kidsnfeet.htm

Visit the KidsNfeet website to print out an easy-to-use shoe measuring system. This printable size ruler will assist you in measuring your children's feet to be sure you get the right fit when shopping for your child's footwear.

✺ Lampkin Design Group
www.fussybaby.net

This website contains free printable images to help calm and stimulate your baby. You can choose "The Slide Show," which consists of several images that will appear on your computer screen for about ten to fifteen seconds each, or "The Poster," which contains images that you can print out. (Bookmark this site to use during those inconsolable moments.)

Little Koala
www.littlekoala.com (click on "Postcards")

Little Koala offers free mother and baby and breast-feeding E-mail postcards from Van Gogh, Rembrandt, Monet, and other famous artists. There is also a place where you can write a personalized message below the postcard.

Maternity Mall
www.maternitymall.com (click on "Baby Names")

Maternity Mall offers a free listing of baby names through an interactive search, as well as a free pregnancy tracker and more.

National Campaign for Hearing Health
www.hearinghealth.net/pages/contact/contact.asp

The National Campaign for Hearing Health focuses on babies and children to make sure that all children have their hearing screened at birth. Visit the website to join the National Campaign for Hearing Health and receive a free infant hearing checklist, a list of hospitals that test newborn hearing, or a free set of earplugs. Be sure to check out the website also for more information on the importance of hearing health. This offer is available to residents of the United States only.

Natrol Nutrition Club
www.natrol.com (click on "Nutrition Club")

Natrol has an extensive line of children's and adults' vitamins, supplements, and formulas. You can join the Natrol Nutrition Club by filling out a brief form at the website. There is no cost to join this club, and as a way of saying thank you for participating, Natrol will send you a Natrol Nutripak, which includes a company brochure, a coupon for the next purchase of any Natrol product, and free sample packets. The Natrol Nutripak is only available to residents of the United States. Residents of Canada who join will benefit from nutrition news and promotional offers.

By joining the Natrol Nutrition Club, you will instantly become eligible to win $100 worth of Natrol products. The contest is open to residents of the United States only. Check out Natrol's website for further contest details.

Parenting.com BabyNamer

www.parenting.com/parenting/tools/babynamer/index.html

Need help finding a name for your baby? This website offers a free BabyNamer where you can check out the meaning of a baby's name, as well as find the top ten boys' and girls' names from 1880 to 2001. Click on "Tools" for the BabyNamer.

Parenting.com Family Creativity Center

www.parenting.com/parenting/partners/hp/new_baby.html

At this website you can print out free baby shower kits, invitations, thank-you cards, and more.

Parents.com Home Emergency Guide

www.parents.com/health/emergency_guides/index.jsp

Parents.com offers a free printable Home Emergency Card (click on "Emergency info to post at home") where you can list important phone numbers and other pertinent information in case of an emergency. Tape this card near your phone or on your refrigerator for your children, baby-sitter, or anyone who may need it. This website also offers a free Travel Emergency Card (click on "Emergency info to carry with you") that you can print out and store in your wallet, glove compartment, or first-aid kit.

❀ ParentsPlace.com Homemade Baby Food Board
boards2.parentsplace.com/cgi-bin/boards/homemadebabyfood

This message board features tons of terrific postings from other parents on making homemade baby food.

❀ Quaker Oatmeal
www.quakeroatmeal.com/toddler/growthchart/offer.cfm

When you sign up at the Quaker Oatmeal website to receive the *Quaker Toddler Newsletter*, you will receive a free growth chart to help you keep track of your child's changing height, as well as a free informational brochure. This growth chart contains a place for your child's name and an area for pictures of your child. This offer is available to residents of the United States and Canada.

❀ Sears Portrait Studio Story Creations
www.searsportrait.com

At the Sears Portrait Studio website you can get a free printable baby book to record all of your baby's firsts. You'll also find countless games and educational activities to make learning fun for your baby, including "story creations," "baby alphabet," "baby count with me," "baby dress-up," and more.

❀ Sesame Street Music Works Video
www.amc-music.com/musicworks/home.htm

To help bring music into your children's lives, Sesame Workshop and NAMM–International Music Products Association are offering a free music video called "Music Works Wonders," which stars Hoots, Elmo, and other Muppet characters. To receive your free music video, complete a brief online survey. This offer is available to residents of the United States only.

❦ Similasan
www.healthyrelief.com

Similasan products provide relief for the eyes, ears, nose, and throat. Similasan eardrops help relieve earaches in children and are safe for all ages. You can download a coupon from the website, which is valid for money off any Similasan product.

❦ TLContact.com
www.tlcontact.com

TLContact.com offers a free CarePage service that will save you from making countless phone calls to relay information to concerned relatives and friends when you're expecting a baby or if you have a child who needs to spend time in the hospital. Visit the site for details on setting up your own personalized webpage, uploading photos, and sharing your news. This offer is available to residents of the United States and Canada.

❦ Totally Toddler
www.totallytoddler.com (click on "Save Money Now!")

Totally Toddler is a nursery stain and odor remover and prewash that is used to remove stains and odors caused by food, baby's spit-up, and formula, as well as messes from bed-wetting, grass, and others. It is non-toxic and safe to use around children and pets. Visit the website to receive a discount on any Totally Toddler product. This offer is available to residents of the United States only.

❦ USA Baby
www.usababy.com/registry/index.html

Complete and submit USA Baby's online form, then print out a coupon that will entitle you to one free teddy bear when you visit a USA Baby store to complete a baby registry. (USA Baby has made this offer available on and off at the website. If the free offer is not currently available, check back again at a later time.) This offer is available to residents of the United States only.

Free Software Downloads for Mom and Baby

The following websites offer free or try-before-you-buy software for you and your baby that is both fun and educational. The try-before-you-buy downloads are free for a limited time only. If you decide you like the software, you can purchase it after the demo period has expired. In any event, all the software downloads I've listed here are free, with no initial cost to you.

Be sure to test out the BabyType software. It's great for babies who just love to bang away on your computer. My three children just loved it!

ABC Color with Me
www.papajan.com (click on "Free Software")

ABC Color with Me is a cute software program where kids can color pictures while listening to lively music. Visit the PapaJan.com website to download a free copy of this software for your little one.

BabyRecon
www.5star-shareware.com (type "BabyRecon" in the Search box)

BabyRecon is a free statistical analysis tool that allows you to discover the sex of your future child, with a high degree of accuracy. Precision forecasts of 89 to 94 percent have been made.

BabyStep
www.babystep.com

At this website you can download the free basic version of BabyStep software. This software contains a pregnancy calendar, a baby book, a photo album, an address book, and more.

❦ Baby Ticker
www.babyticker.com

Baby Ticker was developed to keep friends and family informed of your baby's development and new accomplishments. Baby Ticker includes free baby scrapbook website software where you can record all the significant events in your child's life. Friends and family can visit the website to receive updated baby information by viewing the highlights from your baby scrapbook. Visitors will even be able to download and view video clips of the family! Baby Ticker keeps track of the total number of people who have viewed the website and the date and time of their most recent visit. Check out the website for more details.

❦ BabyToons: Software for Babies and Toddlers
www.zdnet.com/downloads (type "BabyToons" in the Search box)

BabyToons shareware software is a fun program that contains a collection of games designed especially for babies and toddlers aged 10 months to 2½ years. Throughout this program they will learn key concepts such as up/down, happy/sad, colors and shapes, and more. This free download contains four fully functional games that do not expire. If you like the software, you can purchase an additional eight games.

❦ BabyType
www.raize.com/cproducts/babytype/default.htm

At this website you can download a free ten-day demo version of BabyType software for your baby or toddler, perfect for babies and small children who like to bang away on your computer keyboard. With Baby-Type, you can convert your computer into a child's activity center. When your baby presses a key on the keyboard, BabyType plays a sound on the computer's speakers and displays a random shape or the letter corresponding to the key that was pressed on the screen. The free ten-day demo is fully functional, but to continue playing BabyType after the expiration, you must purchase the software.

✿ BabyWatch

www.babiesonline.com/pregnancy/babywatch/content.asp

BabyWatch is a freeware-shareware program to help you "watch" your pregnancy. It contains thousands of baby names that you can browse through, the meaning of the name, the geographic origin of the name, a personality description that often goes with the name, a basic countdown counter, and more. The basic version of BabyWatch is free, but you can order the upgraded version, with additional features, for a fee.

✿ Barnyard Friends

www.5star-shareware.com (type "Barnyard Friends" in the Search box)

Entertain your little one with 123Learn: Barnyard Friends, a free software download featuring assorted farm animals. Your child will enjoy clicking on different things to hear the sounds each animal makes.

✿ Birth Announcement Maker

www.zdnet.com/downloads (type "Birth Announcement Maker" in the Search box)

With the free Birth Announcement Maker demo, you can create your very own custom birth announcements on your home computer and print them out in minutes.

✿ BusyBaby

www.zdnet.com/downloads (type "BusyBaby" in Search box)

BusyBaby is a software that is designed to let your baby play safely on the computer, while teaching him shapes, colors, words, letters, and numbers. The trial version of this software is free but has limited features. If you enjoy the software, you can purchase the full version for a fee.

❀ Child Emergency Profile Service

www.zdnet.com/downloads (type "Child Emergency Profile
   Service" in the Search box)

You can use the free Web-based Child Emergency Profile Service application to securely store your child's vital personal and emergency information.

❀ ChildProof

www.zdnet.com/downloads (type "ChildProof" in the Search box)

Use the ChildProof shareware software to protect your computer and make it safe around kids who might inadvertently erase, delete, rename, or destroy things on the system while it is in use. With Child-Proof, you can build custom play areas that contain games, tools, or educational programs.

❀ Dawn's Due Date Screen Saver

www.dawnsoft.com/dldc.html

Dawn's free Due Date Screen Saver will display your due date and automatically count down the days left until that date. A cute stork picture is displayed with your due date and the number of days that are remaining.

❀ Forest Field Trip

www.5star-shareware.com (type "Forest Field Trip" in the Search
   box)

Your little one can discover all sorts of forest friends with 123Learn: Forest Field Trip, a free software download. She can explore this software by clicking on different things to hear the sounds they make.

✺ Jungle Adventure

www.5star-shareware.com (type "Jungle Adventure" in the Search box)

Your little one can hear all the sounds of the animals in the jungle with 123Learn: Jungle Adventure, a free software download that will take your child on a safari adventure!

✺ Li'lTracks

www.zdnet.com/downloads (type "Li'lTracks" in the Search box)

The Li'lTracks demo will help you to manage and organize your child care business. This software allows you to track and manage payments, account balances, emergency contact information, vaccinations, medical instructions, and other information. With Li'lTracks, you can generate payment receipts, daily attendance sign-in/sign-out rolls, daily child activity reports, and more. It is perfect for a home or center-based child care business. You can download the trial version for free for thirty days.

✺ MomToBe: The Pregnancy Assistant

www.5star-shareware.com (type "MomToBe" in the Search box)

This computerized pregnancy software enables moms-to-be to monitor the various stages of motherhood. It also provides information on how to prepare for pregnancy aimed at those who are at the "just thinking about getting pregnant" stage. When you are trying to get pregnant, the software provides you with a Basal Body Temperature Chart to indicate when you are ovulating, as well as useful information about how best to get pregnant, when the best time is to get pregnant, and more. The "You Are Pregnant" section features a Desktop Weekly Calendar to maintain appointments. "Weekly Information" provides a description of the baby, including its possible weight, height, and more. This software will also help you estimate the due date of your baby. Just for fun, the Chinese Sex Calendar helps identify your baby's sex. The trial version of this program is free but has limited monthly baby information. If you enjoy the software, you can purchase the full version.

❧ Personal Growth Charts
www.zdnet.com/downloads (type "Personal Growth Charts" in the Search box)

This software demo allows you to store, display, and print your child's growth information in a convenient spreadsheetlike format.

❧ Right Time Reader
www.zdnet.com/downloads (type "Right Time Reader" in the Search box)

This free reading program enables you to teach your infant the printed word in the same way that you already do with the spoken word. This program also contains children's books that you can personalize. You can even create your own children's books with this educational program!

❧ S + J's Due Date Calculator
www.zdnet.com/downloads (type "S + J's Due Date Calculator" in the Search box)

S + J's Due Date Calculator measures your estimated due date, calculated on the first day of your last menstrual period. This free software also comes with a month-by-month guide on what to expect during each month of your pregnancy.

❧ Teletubbies Theme Pack and Screensaver
www.kidsdomain.com/down/pc/teletubbtheme.html

Visit this website to download a free, fun, and entertaining Tele-tubbies theme pack and screensaver with bright colors, lively music, and of course—the Teletubbies!

❀ Who Spilled the Tubby Custard?

www.kidsdomain.com/down/pc/tubbycustard.html

This free software download will take your kids on a fun journey with the Teletubbies and help answer the question, "Who spilled the Tubby Custard?" Kids will hear a story and learn new words and sounds.

Free Film Developing, Prints, and Portrait Offers

I think in my babies' first years of life I must have spent more money on pictures than I did on diapers! When I look back on it now, I'm glad I did. Those pictures are so precious!

If you're anything like me, you're probably going to go out and buy tons of rolls of film, and you'll want to have a couple of professional portraits taken as well.

So go ahead, take tons of pictures, and get your adorable little angel all dolled up for a beautiful portrait sitting, while saving money by checking out some of the free offers listed below.

❀ JCPenney Portraits

In the United States, call 800-59-SMILE

www.jcpenneyportraits.com/freebabystuff/

What could be nicer than snuggling your sweet new baby? Nothing really, but free baby stuff is sure a close second. Take advantage of this "Free Stuff" offer to capture special memories of your baby. They grow up before you know it! Receive a free 8 × 10 portrait with no sitting fees ($21.99 value)! Visit the above-listed website for a printable coupon.

This site also shows you how to become a Portrait Club member, providing you with two years of portrait discounts and benefits.

JCPenney Portraits are located in most larger JCPenney stores. Visit their website or call the toll-free number for the location nearest you. This offer is available to residents of the United States only.

❧ Olan Mills

In the United States or Canada, call 800-252-6526
www.olanmills.com/indexd.asp

Olan Mills offers eleven free new baby portraits of children 3 months of age or younger. To register, click on "New Baby?" at the Olan Mills website. Check out the website for other special offers, including a free birthday club, printable discount coupons, and more.

❧ Picture People Clubs

www.picturepeople.com/club/clubs.html

The Picture People have three different clubs that you can join: Smilestones, the Birthday Club, and the Portrait Club. Smilestones, a club for new moms, offers four free portraits for your baby's first year. When you join the Birthday Club, you will receive a free 8 × 10 portrait and a free Baskin-Robbins ice cream cone (with the purchase of the same). The Portrait Club offers unlimited free sittings for the whole family for one full year, three free portrait sheets, and other special savings for members. The cost to join the Portrait Club is $39.95. Smilestones and the Birthday Club are free to join. Visit the website for more details. This offer is available to residents of the United States only.

❧ PictureTrail

www.picturetrail.com/register/register.cgi

When you sign up for your free online PictureTrail account, you will be able to share your photos online with friends and family, upload photos to as many photo albums as you would like, customize each photo album with graphics and background colors, add MIDI music to your albums, and more. Check out the website for further details. This offer is available to residents of the United States and Canada.

❦ Sears Portrait Studio

In the United States or Canada, call 866-292-4949
www.sears-portrait.com

Log on to the website to receive discount coupons to be redeemed
at participating Sears Portrait Studios in the United States (click on
"Coupons") or Canada (click on "Canadian Coupons"). Click on "send
me email specials" to receive E-mail specials on portrait coupon offers
and new contests, as well as to obtain information about Sears Portrait
Studio's free birthday gift to parents with children aged 10 or younger.
This offer is available to residents of the United States and Canada.

❦ Shutterfly

www.shutterfly.com

Shutterfly is a Web-based photo service. When you sign up for a free
membership with Shutterfly, you will receive fifteen free 4 × 6 prints
and free Shutterfly SmartUpload software as well as free picture stor-
age to help you store and organize all of your pictures online. Visit the
website to sign up. This offer is available to residents of the United States
and Canada.

❦ Snapfish

www.snapfish.com

When you sign up with Snapfish, you will receive ten free prints the
first time you upload to your Snapfish account. Snapfish will also develop
your first roll of film free of charge. All you pay is $1.99 for shipping
and handling of your prints and negatives. Check out the website for
more details. Film processing services are available to residents of the
United States only. However, residents of Canada are free to view albums
and upload digital pictures.

Free Stuff from Stores

Many department stores, chain stores, and grocery stores that carry infant wear, maternity wear, and other baby-related merchandise offer free gifts, parenting packs, baby clubs, and discounts to new and expecting moms. Some stores offer discounts for parents of multiples, some will offer free gifts for you and your baby when you register with them, and others give away valuable discount coupons and free samples of brand-name baby products for you to try out.

The best thing that you can do when visiting a store that carries infant wear and other baby-related merchandise is to ask what special offers they have available for new and expecting parents. Keep in mind that many store clerks may feel uncomfortable in pointing out that you are pregnant, especially if you are in the early months, and may hesitate approaching you with their company's offers. Make a point of asking wherever you go to be sure you don't miss out on anything!

The following is a list of stores for you to check out when you're out shopping for your little one.

Drop-In Freebies

If you find any of the following stores in your neighborhood, consider yourself lucky! Drop into any of these stores to receive all kinds of terrific freebies, including free gifts, money-saving coupons, free promotional items for yourself and your baby, as well as the opportunity to sign up for various programs, clubs, and baby registries.

❧ Acme Baby Club
www.acmemarkets.com/acme/babyclub.asp

For every dollar you spend on baby products at Acme Markets, you will earn one Baby Point. When you collect 100 Baby Points with your Acme SuperCard, you will receive a $10 gift card. You can apply for a free Acme SuperCard at the courtesy counter at any Acme store location. See the website for further details. This offer is available to residents of the United States only.

❧ Acme Markets
www.acmemarkets.com/acme/specials/birthdaycake.asp

To receive a free birthday cake when your child's first birthday arrives, bring a copy of his or her birth certificate to a bakery associate at any participating Acme Market. This offer is available only in Acme stores with a bakery department and is available to residents of the United States only.

❧ Babies "R" Us and Toys "R" Us
www.babiesrus.com

When you visit any Babies "R" Us or Toys "R" Us store to register your baby shower, you will receive free gifts, money-saving coupons, and other free promotional items. You can visit any store location to register, or register at the website. This offer is available to residents of the United States only.

❧ Baby Depot
In the United States, call 888-BCF-COAT
www.coat.com

The Baby Depot has a gift registry for expecting parents. Stop by any store location to register. This offer is available to residents of the United States only.

❦ Eckerd BabyCare Club

In the United States, call 800-325-3737

www.eckerd.com (click on "Baby Care")

Members of the Eckerd BabyCare Club will receive a free membership card in the mail, along with valuable coupons. Members will also receive 10 percent off infant formulas and accessories, children's prescriptions, baby items, the *Talking Babies* newsletter, and more. Visit the website to fill out the online enrollment form to join the free club, or visit store location to enroll. Call the toll-free number for further details. This offer is available to residents of the United States only.

❦ Meijer

www.meijer.com/babyclub

Expectant parents and anyone with children under the age of 3 can join the Meijer Baby Club. When you join this free club, you will receive useful information and savings. Meijer also offers a free baby gift registry where you can register your baby shower with them. Visit one of the Meijer store locations to register, or register online. Check out the website for further details. This offer is available to residents of the United States only.

❦ OshKosh B'Gosh

www.oshkoshbgosh.com

Parents of multiples will receive a special 10 percent discount on their purchase when they visit an OshKosh B'Gosh store location to register for the multiples program. This offer is available to residents of the United States only.

❦ Payless ShoeSource
www.payless.com

Drop in with your beautiful new baby and register at any Payless ShoeSource store to get a free pair of baby shoes. There are three styles to choose from: pink, blue denim, or white!

❦ Publix Baby Club
In the United States, call 863-688-7407 (x8700)

The Publix Baby Club is available to expectant parents, and families with children up to 24 months. When you join the Publix Baby Club, you will receive coupons for free baby products, an A-Z baby book published by the American Academy of Pediatrics, a free newsletter, and more. Pick up an enrollment form in the baby aisle or at the customer service desk of any Publix Super Market, or call the Publix Baby Club Member Message Line to request more information. This offer is available to residents of the United States only.

❦ Sears
In the United States, call 800-349-4358
In Canada, call, 800-211-2111
In the United States: www.sears.com
In Canada: www.sears.ca

The following are various free programs offered to new and expecting parents when they attend at participating Sears department stores.

- **Sears Request Baby Registry:** When you visit any Sears location to register your baby shower, you will receive a free gift. You can sign up for your gift registry at the in-store Sears Request kiosk at any Sears location. This offer is available to residents of the United States and Canada.

- **Waiting Game Club** (www.sears.ca): Drop in at any Sears infants' department, or go online to register for the Waiting Game for expectant mothers who have signed up for the Sears Request Baby Registry, as described in the listing mentioned previously. If you are expecting and can correctly guess the due date of your baby, you will receive all of the Sears baby purchases that you have made through your Baby Registry absolutely free! To be eligible for this contest, your birth must be a natural birth, and you must sign up for the contest at least sixty days before your expected due date. Visit any Sears infants' department for details. The Waiting Game is available to residents of Canada only.

- **Sears KidVantage Club:** Drop in at any Sears children's or infants' department for details on the KidVantage Club. This club offers the Wear Out Warranty. If your infant's or child's clothing or shoes wear out before they're outgrown, Sears will replace the clothing or shoes free in the same size. This offer is available to residents of the United States and Canada. Residents of the United States who join the Kid-Vantage Club will also earn a 15 percent shopping discount off of their next infants' or children's apparel purchase for every $100 (U.S.) that they spend on Sears clothing.

- **Sears Family First Club** (In Canada, call 800-265-3675; www.sears .ca/e/serv/famfirst.htm): When you sign up for the exclusive Sears Family First Club, you will receive savings on merchandise and services at Sears, including a membership kit containing over $500 in coupon savings, a Kraft recipe booklet, a complimentary safety ID kit from Sears Portrait Studio, savings on family vacations and hotels, events, as well as additional savings throughout the year. You will also receive the *Sears Family First Magazine*, a fun and education full-color guide that includes family fun ideas, health and fashion information, and recipes, as well as additional savings coupons. The cost to join this club is $24.99 (a $1,000 value). Drop into any Sears kids wear or toy department, or call the above-listed number to register. This club is available to residents of Canada only.

Toys "R" Us

In Canada, call 800-TOYS-R-US
www.toysrus.com

When you visit any Toys "R" Us store to register your baby shower in the Babies "R" Us department, you will receive a free parenting starter kit filled with baby essentials, as well as free discount coupons. You will also be added to a mailing list to receive free baby catalogs periodically throughout the year, with additional valuable coupons offering further savings. This offer is available to residents of Canada only.

USA Baby
www.usababy.com

Parents of multiples can drop in at any USA Baby store to receive 10 percent off the sale price of their second duplicate item.

Grocery Store Baby Clubs

Grocery store clubs are popping up everywhere, offering all kinds of programs where you can collect points to save money on baby products and other store merchandise when you shop at these stores. Some of these clubs even offer instant cash-back rewards.

In this section I have listed only a portion of the grocery stores that offer free "new parent" or "baby clubs." When shopping at your local grocery store, be sure to ask if there is a program available for parents. Many stores do have these clubs available, but you may just not be aware of them.

A&P Baby Bonus Clubs (Canada)
A&P stores in Canada: A&P, Dominion, Ultra Food & Drug
In Canada, call 877-76-FRESH
www.freshobsessed.com

The Baby Bonus Club is an exclusive program of A&P, Dominion, and Ultra Food & Drug stores. You can earn Baby Bonus Club Points on more than twelve hundred items throughout the store when you present your Air Miles card to the cashier at the front desk. When you accumulate ten points, you will receive a $20 gift certificate. Baby Bonus Club Points are in addition to any regular or bonus Air Miles Reward Miles you earn. To apply, simply go to any participating A&P, Dominion, or Ultra Food & Drug location. Call or visit the website for further details. This program is available at participating A&P stores only. There may be variations in the club program from store to store.

A&P Baby Bonus Clubs (U.S.)
A&P stores in the United States: A&P, Waldbaum's, SuperFresh, Sav-A-Center, Farmer Jack
www.aptea.com (click on store logo)

Various A&P stores throughout the United States offer a free Baby Bonus Club to their shoppers. As a club member, you will receive $20 instant cash-back every time you spend $200 in baby item purchases using a Bonus Savings Club card. There is no limit to the number of times you can qualify for your $20 cash-back reward. Look for the Baby Bonus Club shelf tags at participating grocery stores to earn free Baby Bonus Points on more than nine hundred items every week. You can apply for a Bonus Savings Club card by filling out an application available on the website that you can print out and bring to the courtesy counter at participating A&P locations, or simply visit a participating A&P location to apply. Many of these stores also have signs throughout their store that will show you additional savings on numerous other items for club members. When at the checkout counter, simply present your club card to the cashier, and the discounts and coupon savings will be automatically deducted from your total bill. This program is available at participating A&P stores only. There may be variations in the Baby Bonus Club program from store to store.

ShopRite Baby Bucks
www.shoprite.com/babybucks/intro.htm

When you sign up for the ShopRite Baby Bucks program, you will automatically get $5 off your next shopping order of $50 or more when you spend $50 on baby items at any ShopRite location. Stop in and visit any ShopRite store location to register. You can also register online if you prefer. This offer is available to residents of the United States only.

❦ Smith's Baby Fresh Reward Points Program
In the United States, call 800-764-8897
www.smithsfoodanddrug.com/savings_freshvalues_babyfresh
    _1.htm

For every dollar you spend on baby items (including diapers and formula) at Smith's Food & Drug Stores, you will earn one point when you use your Fresh Values card. When you sign up for a Fresh Values card, you will save $10 on your groceries every time you accumulate two hundred Baby Fresh Reward points. You will also receive fifty free Baby Fresh Reward points when you sign up for the Smith's Baby Fresh Rewards Program. As a member of the Baby Fresh Rewards Program, you will also be entitled to receive a free can of powdered infant formula for every eight cans that you buy, a free birthday cake to help you celebrate your little one's first birthday, special manufacturers' coupons and other offers and discounts—even free cookies from the bakeshop for your child! Visit your local Smith's Food & Drug Store to register, or call for further details. This offer is available to residents of the United States only.

❦ Tom Thumb Stork Club
www.tomthumb.com/promotions.asp

When you join the Tom Thumb Stork Club, you will receive valuable coupons for you and your baby, as well as up-front parking, effective three months prior to and three months after the birth of your baby. Visit any Tom Thumb store location to register at the courtesy booth. This offer is available to residents of the United States only.

Wegmans Baby Care Club

In the United States or Canada, call 800-WEGMANS (ext. 4760)
www.wegmans.com (click on "Enjoy the Benefits!")

Parents can register online to join the Wegmans Baby Care Club and receive quarterly mailings with discount coupons and more. This club is free to join and open to all Shoppers Club Members. It is available to expectant parents and for parents with children up to 3 years of age. You can also visit a Wegmans store to fill out a registration form. Stop by any store location or check the website for details. This offer is available to residents of the United States only.

Free Parenting Books, Magazines, and Other Literature

Shortly after you give birth, the nurse at the hospital hands you your beautiful bundle of joy, all wrapped up in a blanket and smelling sweet and new after his very first bath. A soft smile crosses your face as you exchange loving glances with your husband. Next, your eyes slowly move back down to your beautiful new baby once again. Ahhh . . . what an angel! But suddenly you realize, as you glance around the hospital room in a panic, that you've been left alone with this darling little infant. Your husband jumps up. "What, no instructions?!" you hear him yell, as he desperately runs up and down the halls to find the nearest available nurse.

I bought a new TV last week, and it came with instructions. My new VCR came with instructions. Even an electric can opener comes with instructions. Help!

I think all new parents feel a certain amount of anxiety or even panic after their baby is first born: "What if I do something wrong?" "What do I do when the baby starts to cry?" "What if I can't remember how to change a diaper?" Don't worry. These feelings are completely natural.

As a new parent, you want to do what is best for your baby. The terrific parenting books, magazines, and literature that I have listed in this chapter are available to educate you in all areas of your pregnancy, child-birth, and the care of your baby, as well as to help give you the confidence you need to be the best parent you can be.

When in doubt, keep in mind the wise words of Dr. Spock, a beloved father, author, and pediatrician who influenced millions of parents around the world: "Trust yourself. You know more than you think you do."

Parenting Books

The following free books are exceptional—must-haves for all new moms and moms-to-be! They cover pregnancy, childbirth, child care, health and nutrition, and many other important topics of parenting.

❧ Family Communications Inc.
In Canada, call 416-537-2604 (sorry, not a toll-free number)

Call to receive a free 178-page reference book titled *The New Quick Reference Baby and Child Care Encyclopaedia*, rated by four hundred Canadian doctors to be the best single source of child care information. This book is a special gift from the publishers of *Best Wishes* magazine and is free for a limited time only. This offer is available to residents of Canada only.

❧ State Farm Insurance
In the United States or Canada, call 888-733-8368

Call to receive *Mayo Clinic Complete Book of Pregnancy and Baby's First Year* for free. This comprehensive 712-page hardcover book guides you through each phase of pregnancy, birth, and baby's exciting and important first year. This offer is available to residents of the United States and Canada.

Parenting Magazines

There are a lot of great parenting magazines on the market today, with so much terrific parenting information and advice. I actually subscribed to three of them when I was expecting and devoured every page. The articles were always up-to-date and provided tons of entertainment, information, and resources for new or expecting parents.

Following are some of the top parenting magazines on the market today, including *Parents, Parenting, Today's Parent, American Baby,* and *Baby Talk.* Many of these magazine offers are absolutely free. And for others, you can receive a free trial issue to give you a chance to decide if you would like to subscribe further. Your first issue is always free, and you can cancel any further issues, if you wish. So if you're not sure which parenting magazine you would like to subscribe to, here's a great chance to try them out for free!

❦ American Baby

www.americanbaby.com (click on "Free Offers")

For some sixty-five years, *American Baby* magazine has been the most trusted source of information for new or expectant parents. It features helpful articles on every area of parenting, including health, development, and nutrition. Every issue offers money-saving coupons for brand-name baby products. For a free subscription to *American Baby* magazine, sign up online. This offer is available to residents of the United States only.

❦ Baby Talk

In the United States, call 800-395-1976

www.parenting.com/parenting/magazines/babytalk.html

Baby Talk is America's number one magazine for your baby's first year of life. It contains information for new or expectant parents. Your subscription for ten issues is absolutely free, no strings attached. Call or register online to begin your free subscription. This offer is available to residents of the United States only.

❧ March of Dimes
1275 Mamaroneck Avenue
White Plains, NY 10605
In the United States or Canada, call 888-663-4637
www.marchofdimes.com/aboutus/request_form.asp

The March of Dimes offers *Mama: Your Guide to a Healthy Pregnancy* free of charge. *Mama* is an award-winning magazine for pregnant women and new moms. It contains practical and fun information for parents-to-be, including articles on pregnancy planning, nutrition, growth and development, and more.

To order, call or order directly at the March of Dimes website. This offer is available to residents of the United States and Canada.

❧ *Parenting*
www.parenting.com/parenting

Parenting magazine offers tons of parenting articles; information on newborn care, nutrition, and outdoor activities; delicious recipes; health and safety tips; and more. Log on to this website to get a free preview issue of *Parenting* magazine. This offer is available to residents of the United States and Canada. You can also click on "Free Magazines" at the website to get a free subscription offer from *Baby Talk* magazine (United States only). Click on "Free Newsletters" to sign up for free pregnancy and baby newsletters.

❧ *Parents*
In the United States, call 800-727-3682 (ext. 2521)
www.parents.com (click on "Get Your Risk-Free Issue Here!")

Parents magazine delivers reliable child care advice and helps to make raising your baby easier, more fun, and more rewarding. Residents of the United States and Canada can register online to receive a free trial issue of *Parents* magazine. Residents of the United States can also call to order as well.

❦ *S-Magazine*

U.S. website: www.s-mag.com

Canadian website: www.s-mag.com/canada/index.html

Procter & Gamble's *S-Magazine* is an electronic magazine geared toward moms to help simplify their lives, based on value-added content, tips, tools, and brand-specific solutions. A popular section of the magazine is the "Offer Corner" where consumers can sign up to receive advertised offers from Procter & Gamble and other companies. For a free subscription to *S-Magazine*, click on "Subscribe."

❦ *Taking Good Care*

In the United States, call 877-244-5332

Call to sign up for the Sesame Street Goes to the Doctor Program, funded by Pfizer, from the Children's Television Workshop. When you sign up for this program, you will receive a special edition of *Sesame Street Parent's Magazine* titled *Taking Good Care*, which includes a bright Elmo poster. This magazine explains how antibiotics should be used wisely, how to help children with common illnesses, how to alleviate fear when children go to the doctor, and other health-related information. This offer is available to residents of the United States only.

❦ *Today's Parent*

In Canada, call 800-567-8697

www.todaysparent.com

Today's Parent is a Canadian magazine for parents of children from birth to 12 years of age. The magazine offers informative articles on parenting issues, health and safety concerns, lifestyle, and food and nutrition, as well as information on child development and behavior. Call or log on to the *Today's Parent* website for information about how you can receive a free issue.

Today's Parent offers two additional free magazines to parents who are expecting: *Pregnancy and Birth* and *Newborn*. These excellent prenatal and postnatal publications are available free of charge at most doctors' offices. Ask for a free copy at your next prenatal or postnatal visit.

These offers are available to residents of Canada only.

❀ Twins

> In the United States or Canada, call 800-328-3211
> www.twinsmagazine.com

Twins magazine is dedicated to making life more enjoyable and easier for parents of multiples. The magazine contains birth stories, tips on raising multiples, and more. Call to receive a risk-free trial issue of *Twins: The Magazine for Parents of Multiples*, or download a free issue from the website. This offer is available to residents of the United States and Canada.

❀ Welcome Home

> In the United States or Canada, call 866-352-1075
> www.familyandhome.org (click on "Subscribe," then "Sample
> Issue")

This advertisement-free, award-winning journal supports mothers and fathers who choose to be at home to nurture their families. It contains informative articles, essays, and more. Visit the website to view a free sample issue. You can also call to order a free information packet and free sample. This offer is available to residents of the United States and Canada.

Other Parenting Literature

The educational pamphlets and brochures discussed in the following section cover many parenting topics, including child safety, breast-feeding tips and advice, postpartum depression, medical concerns, nutrition, and your baby's development—and of course, they're free!

✾ Best Start Resource Centre
www.opc.on.ca/beststart/Early_Years (click on order form)

The Best Start Resource Centre offers tons of free resource packages for new or expecting moms. You can download the HTML versions of these resources online or order the printed version of these resources by filling out the online order form. These resources are available to residents of Canada only.

The following resource packages are available free of charge (a small shipping and handling fee applies):

- *Alcohol and Drug Use During Pregnancy.* This fact sheet addresses how alcohol and other drugs can affect the baby, what pregnant women should avoid, and other related issues.

- *Breastfeeding Is Best Feeding.* This information sheet describes the benefits of breast-feeding both to you and your baby.

- *Butt It Out.* "Tobacco smoke is the biggest cause of small unhealthy babies. Women planning a pregnancy should quit smoking and avoid secondhand smoke to give their babies the best start possible in life." This information sheet discusses the impact of smoking on your unborn baby. It lists tips to help you quit smoking as well.

- *The Early Years Primer.* This prenatal resource booklet contains valuable information for expectant parents. It includes a quiz to help women think about their pregnancy and help encourage women to talk to their health care provider as openly as possible.

- *Eat Healthy, Eat Well!* This information sheet discusses some of the healthy choices that you can make to have the healthiest baby possible.

- *Folic Acid.* This free resource package contains an informational paper and a video to make women of childbearing years aware of the need to take folic acid every day to reduce their chances, should they become pregnant, of having a baby with a neural tube defect. This package includes articles on folic acid, a folic acid quiz, and more.

- *Health Before Pregnancy.* The purpose of this resource is to educate people about the possible influence that lifestyle choices and health status can have on conception, pregnancy, and birth outcomes, as well as to promote changes that people can make to improve their health before becoming pregnant. This resource package contains tons of great resources, including informational papers and articles, as well as a free video.

- *Physical Activity and Pregnancy.* This fact sheet discusses whether women should exercise during pregnancy. It also gives general guidelines for exercising safely during pregnancy.

- *Prevention of Preterm Birth.* This resource package includes an informational paper and educational video that addresses the signs and symptoms of preterm labor. It is filled with strategic tips and guidelines to help you to more effectively respond to the signs and symptoms of preterm birth.

- *Nutrition and Pregnancy.* This fact sheet addresses the following questions: How does the mother's nutrition affect the baby? What is the recommended weight gain during pregnancy? When should a pregnant woman seek help with her diet?

- *Social Support During Pregnancy.* This fact sheet addresses the importance of a mother receiving social support during her pregnancy. It also addresses the effects that stress can have on a baby, what a woman should do if she is feeling stressed or isolated, and other related issues.

- *Work and Pregnancy.* This fact sheet describes the type of work that can increase the risk of low birth weight, what a pregnant woman can do to decrease the risk to herself and her baby, how exposure to toxic substances at work might be associated with low birth weight or birth defects and what you can do to prevent such exposures, as well as healthy lifestyle practices that you can adopt at work. There is also a section that lists what employers and employees can do to promote a healthy and safe workplace.

Child Care Aware

1319 F Street NW
Suite 500
Washington, DC 20004-1106
In the United States or Canada, call 800-424-2246
www.childcareaware.org

Child Care Aware is committed to helping families find the highest quality child care and child care resources in their community. Families can call or go online to be directly connected to the Child Care Resource and Referral agency within their own community.

The following free parenting publications are available online or by calling:

- *All in the Family—Making Child Care Provided by Relatives Work for Your Family.* If you are planning on using relatives to care for your child while you work or go to school, read this brochure to help make this a good choice for you, your child, and the relative caring for your child.

- *Child Care Resource and Referral in Your Local Community.* Child Care Resource and Referral services are available in most local communities, providing many valuable services to families. This tip sheet describes what your local Child Care Resource and Referral program can do for you.

- *Choosing Quality Child Care for a Child with Special Needs.* There are important factors to consider when choosing quality child care for a child with special needs. This brochure provides parents with information to help them choose quality child care for their special needs child.

- *Five Steps to Choosing Safe and Healthy Child Care.* When choosing child care for your child, you want to be sure to select a setting that is both safe and healthy. This brochure provides guidelines for families in choosing safe and healthy child care in various settings.

- *Five Steps to Choosing Summer Child Care.* This brochure provides parents with guidelines for choosing a quality summer care program for their child.

- *Give Your Child Something That Will Last a Lifetime . . . Quality Child Care!* This brochure provides parents with helpful steps to choosing quality child care, as well as a checklist to use when choosing a child care home or center.

- *Matching Your Infant's or Toddler's Style to the Right Child Care Setting.* This brochure offers information on how to use what you know about your infant or toddler, like personal style and activity level, to help you select a child care setting that's just right for your child.

❀ Depression After Delivery, Inc.
In the United States or Canada, call 800-944-4773
www.depressionafterdelivery.com

Depression After Delivery provides support for women with ante- and postpartum depression. Call and leave your name and address to receive a free information packet about postpartum depression. This information packet is available to women after childbirth to help them deal with postpartum blues and depression. This offer is available to residents of the United States and Canada.

❀ Dorel Juvenile Group
www.coscoinc.com/services/brochures/brochures.html

Go online to download a free *Travel with Baby* brochure targeting car safety, as well as the *Travel Time* brochure, which contains information regarding strollers and how to select one that is perfect for your needs.

❧ FamilyCare

www.familycareproducts.com/guidebook.asp

Log on to this website to receive the free Recovery Zone guidebook *Mommy, I Don't Feel Good*. This guidebook will teach you how to set up a comfortable place in your home to nurture your child back to health when she isn't feeling well. This offer is available to residents of the United States only.

❧ Ferring Inc.

In Canada, call 800-970-4224
www.bedwetting.ferring.ca

Ferring offers solutions to help with your child's bed-wetting problem. Call for free information about bed-wetting or to talk to a registered nurse. Residents of Canada can call the information line 24/7.

❧ First Response

www.1stresponse.com/brochures/stepstopregnancy.asp

First Response, Steps to Pregnancy is an informative brochure that provides parents with important information on planning a pregnancy. This brochure also contains coupons for First Response Ovulation and Pregnancy Test Kits. You can order this brochure online. This offer is available to residents of the United States only.

❧ Growing Child, Inc.

www.growingchild.com

Growing Child is a child development newsletter that is sent to parents each month. It is timed to the monthly age of your child. This newsletter is available to parents of children age 6 or younger. You can download a free sample issue of *Growing Child*. This offer is available to residents of the United States and Canada.

❦ Juvenile Products Manufacturers Association

JPMA Public Information

17000 Commerce Parkway

Suite C

Mt. Laurel, NJ 08054

www.jpma.org (type "safe and sound for baby" in
the Search box)

The free sixteen-page brochure *Safe & Sound for Baby* illustrates the proper use of many juvenile products, including car seats, changing tables, cribs, crib toys and pacifiers, infant bedding, carriers and swings, carriages and strollers, high chairs, gates and enclosures, infant seats, and more. The brochure also provides safety information on bathing and feeding, household dangers, electrocution, suffocation, and strangulation. For a free copy of this brochure, send a self-addressed, stamped business-size envelope to Juvenile Products Manufacturers Association. Be sure to affix the proper U.S. postage. A downloadable version of this brochure can be found at the website. This offer is available to residents of the United States and Canada.

❦ La Leche League International

In the United States, call 847-519-9585 (sorry, not a toll-free
number)

La Leche League offers two free booklets on breast-feeding: *Breast-feeding and Working: An Important Part of the Active Mother's Balancing Act* and *Practical Hints for Working and Breastfeeding*. These booklets are available for mothers who work outside the home and may have concerns about how best to continue breast-feeding. These booklets answer questions such as "When should I introduce bottles?" "How do I express milk?" "How often will I need to pump at work?" Other issues relating to working moms and breast-feeding are also covered. Call to order these free booklets. This offer is available to residents of the United States only.

❦ March of Dimes

1275 Mamaroneck Avenue
White Plains, NY 10605
In the United States or Canada, call 888-663-4637
mama.modimes.org (click on "Free Materials")

Call or visit their website to obtain the following materials:

- *Are You Ready? A Guide to Planning a Healthy, Happy Pregnancy*. This booklet helps parents-to-be ask and answer tough questions: Are you ready physically to have a baby? Are you ready emotionally? Are you ready financially? This booklet will also help you calculate your due date and give you advice on what to do once you're pregnant, as well as list some things that dads can do during your pregnancy. It also includes advice on getting pregnant, choosing a health care provider, and breaking unhealthy habits. In addition, it features a worksheet for keeping track of important information, such as dates and phone numbers.

- *Genetic Counseling*. This twelve-page booklet shows how family histories and testing can predict many birth defects. It answers questions about genetics and inherited traits, genes, and chromosomes and provides information about testing genetic conditions. It also explains how genetic counseling can help. A family tree is included.

❦ McGraw-Hill Children's Publishing

In the United States or Canada, call 800-417-3261
www.mhkids.com

Call or sign up at McGraw-Hill's website to receive a free bimonthly educational *Parent Newsletter*, as well as to receive free product catalogs, including *McGraw-Hill Children's Publishing Parent Catalog*, *McGraw-Hill Children's Publishing Homeschool Catalog*, or *McGraw-Hill Children's Publishing Christian Educator Catalog*. These colorful catalogs feature tons of educational books, children's storybooks, toys, puzzles, learning materials, and more. This offer is available to residents of the United States and Canada.

❦ Nissan
In the United States or Canada, call 800-955-4500

Call the Nissan Quest for Safety Helpline to receive a free *What to Expect Guide to Car Seat Safety* booklet, which offers information on choosing the right type of car seat, on when to switch to a front-facing seat, and on how long a child should be in a booster seat, along with other car seat safety information. This offer is available to residents of the United States and Canada.

❦ PregnancyWeekly.com
www.pregnancyweekly.com

Sign up for a free electronic newsletter that will support you through a happy, healthy pregnancy.

❦ Safe Kids Canada
180 Dundas Street West
Suite 2105
Toronto, Ontario M5G 1Z8
In Canada, call 888-SAFETIPS
www.safekidscanada.ca

According to Safe Kids Canada, "Injuries are the number one cause of death and disability among Canadian children." Safe Kids Canada is a national charity dedicated to providing parents and children with the information they need to reduce the number of injuries to children across Canada. Call or write to receive free professional literature on childhood injury prevention. This offer is available to residents of Canada only.

❦ **Sharn, Inc.**
In the United States or Canada, call 800-325-3671
www.sharn.com

Call for the free brochure *Tips About Giving Your Baby Medicine*. This offer is available to residents of the United States and Canada.

❦ **Tiny Love**
In the United States or Canada, call 888-TINY-LOVE
www.tinylove.com (click on "Free Developmental Booklet")

Tiny Love makes soft developmental toys made of high-quality material. Call or visit the website to request a free catalog and *Your Baby's Development Guide*, a colorful booklet containing useful information about child development from birth to 24 months. The booklet is arranged by age and developmental element.

Tiny Love also has a "Buy 1, Get 1 Free" Program for parents of twins, triplets, quadruplets, or higher on the first order placed with Tiny Love. Ask for details.

These offers are available to residents of the United States and Canada.

❦ **Toy Industry Association**
Attn: Toy Safety
1115 Broadway
Suite 400
New York, NY 10010
In the United States, call: 877-4TOYSAFETY
www.toy-tia.org/consumer/parents/safety/4toysafety.html

The Toy Industry Association represents more than 250 manufacturers and importers of toys. The Toy Industry Association, under the Toy Industry Foundation's consumer education program, distributes a free booklet titled *Fun Play, Safe Play*, which has general information about safe play and toy safety, as well as an age-by-age guide to buying toys. Write or go online to order a free copy of this booklet. You can also call the toy safety hotline for toy safety tips and advice, as well as to have your questions answered about specific toys. This offer is available to residents of the United States only.

❦ Underwriters Laboratories

In the United States, call 877-UL-4-SAFE

Call for a free room-by-room home safety checklist and other home safety tips. This offer is available to residents of the United States only.

❦ Viacord

In the United States, call 866-565-2221
In Canada, call 866-668-4895
www.viacord.com

Umbilical cord blood may be a component of future therapy for your baby or an immediate family member, as it is rich in stem cells, which can be used in the treatment of many different cancers, genetic diseases, blood disorders, and immune deficiencies. Thanks to medical advances, your newborn's cord blood can be preserved at delivery to potentially treat more than forty-five life-threatening diseases where an umbilical cord blood stem cell transplant may be appropriate. Call today for your free cord blood information kit. This offer is available to residents of the United States and Canada.

❦ Zero to Three

In the United States, call 877-565-5465
In Canada, call 314-216-3560 (sorry, not a toll-free number)
www.zerotothree.org/magic/main.html

The Magic of Everyday Moments Campaign, developed in partnership by Zero to Three and the Johnson & Johnson Pediatric Institute, is designed to help you and other caregivers understand and gain ideas for how to use simple, everyday moments to promote your child's social, emotional, and intellectual development. The Magic of Everyday Moments booklets show parents how everyday activities can be meaningful opportunities to connect with their children. You can download the set of five booklets at no charge. Or you can call to order hard copies of these booklets, but there is a shipping and handling fee of $6 (U.S.) for all five booklets.

Following are the five booklets offered:

- *The Magic of Everyday Moments (0–4 Months)*. This booklet discusses the things that your baby needs most, how to read your baby's cues, comforting your newborn, what it's like for you as a parent, and more.

- *The Magic of Everyday Moments (4–6 Months)*. This booklet discusses what you might be experiencing, feeding your baby, playing with your baby, reading your baby's cues, and more.

- *The Magic of Everyday Moments (6–9 Months)*. This booklet discusses what you might be experiencing through this period, bath time, saying "good night," what your baby needs most, and more.

- *The Magic of Everyday Moments (9–12 Months)*. Topics discussed in this booklet include "Hellos" and "Goodbyes," grocery shopping, reading your baby's cues, what it's like for you as the parent, and more.

- *The Magic of Everyday Moments (12–15 Months)*. This booklet discusses what it's like for you during this toddler period, taking a walk, reading to your baby, and more.

Free Maternity, Baby Wear, and Baby Product Catalogs

Being a busy mom, you might not always have the time to head out to the mall to make purchases for your baby.

When things get really busy and you'd rather stay home than face hordes of shoppers at the mall, consider ordering from a catalog. It can be a simple and convenient way to shop, definitely saving you time and often money, as many of these catalog companies don't have all the overhead costs of running an actual store and can afford to list their prices lower than competitors' prices.

The following companies offer free catalogs that carry tons of products for you or your baby, including a great assortment of adorable baby outfits, practical nursing wear, lots of baby and nursery accessories, and more.

Anna Cris Maternity

In the United States or Canada, call 800-281-ANNA
www.annacris.com

Anna Cris Maternity offers maternity clothes for your career and maternity apparel for your casual weekends, as well as maternity wear

for holidays and special occasions. Call for a free maternity wear catalog. This offer is available to residents of the United States and Canada.

 Avent America, Inc.
In the United States or Canada, call 800-54-AVENT
www.aventamerica.com

Call Avent for a free brochure featuring bottle and breast-feeding
products. This offer is available to residents of the United States and
Canada.

 Baby BumbleBee
In the United States or Canada, call 888-984-5500
www.babybumblebee.com/v2/pages/receive_mail.cfm

Baby BumbleBee provides parents with educationally appropriate
materials for infants and toddlers, including educational videos and
more. You can order a free catalog by calling or by filling out the online
request form. This offer is available to residents of the United States and
Canada.

 Baby Catalog of America
In the United States, call 800-PLAYPEN
www.babycatalog.com (click on "Online Store," then "Search
    Catalog")

Guaranteeing the lowest advertised prices, the Baby Catalog of
America offers everything you'll need for your baby from birth through
the toddler stage, including name-brand monitors, toys, books, strollers,
car seats, crib and twin bedding, nursery decor, and more. You'll get discounts from 10 to 50 percent off pregnancy, baby, and toddler products,
regardless of whether you shop online or over the phone. Residents of
the United States can call to order a free printed catalog. Residents of
the United States and Canada can view the entire catalog online.

This company also has a baby shower and gift registry. Shower guests can buy online and view what has been previously purchased. Check out the website for details.

For a $25 (U.S.) fee, customers can sign up to join the Baby Club to save an additional 10 percent on most purchases. Again, check out the website for details.

This company has an outlet store in West Haven, Connecticut, that carries everything from the website plus more!

❦ Baby Holder

In the United States, call 800-637-9426
In Canada, call 949-361-1089 (sorry, not a toll-free number)
www.babyholder.com

Call for a free catalog of nursing clothes, bras, nighties, breast pumps, and more. A free instructional video is included.

❦ Babystyle

In the United States, call 877-ESTYLES
www.babystyle.com

Call or visit the website to order a free Babystyle catalog featuring the latest in maternity fashions plus toys, gifts, clothing, and other essentials for your baby. This offer is available to residents of the United States only.

Babystyle also offers a convenient baby registry with an automatic "Thank-You" list that keeps track of who gave you what and when. Check out the website for details.

❦ Born to Love

In the United States or Canada, call 905-725-2559 (sorry, not a toll-free number)
www.borntolove.com (click on "Catalogue")

At Born to Love, you will find everything you need for your newborn. There is a large assortment of diapers and diapering accessories, as well as tons of sewing patterns that you can order, including sewing patterns for a baby's layette, toy patterns, patterns to make your own car seat cover, hat and mitten patterns, infant clothing patterns, and more. Residents of the United States and Canada can view the catalog online or order a free catalog by calling.

Born to Love also offers a Catalogue Request Center at www .borntolove.com/catalogues.html. At this website, you can request that an assortment of catalogs from different companies be forwarded to you free of charge. Among the other companies whose catalogs you can choose from are Babyworks, Miracle Baby, Parentsline News, and Natural Baby. This offer is available to residents of the United States and Canada.

❦ Combi International

In the United States, call 800-992-6624
www.combi-intl.com/combi/catalog.htm

To receive a free catalog from Combi with a listing of baby products, including strollers, high chairs, and other baby accessories, call or fill out the form at the website. Catalogs are available to residents of the United States only.

❦ Dorel Juvenile Group

www.djgusa.com/maincat.html

The Dorel Juvenile Group offers three product catalogs that you can view online. The Cosco catalog features strollers, car seats, high chairs, cribs and beds, and more. The Safety 1st catalog features a wide assortment of childproofing and infant health care products. The Eddie Bauer catalog features convertible car seats, auto booster seats, strollers, and play yards.

❦ Ecobaby Organics
In the United States or Canada, call 888-326-2229
www.ecobaby.com (click on "Free Catalog")

To receive a free catalog filled with information on breast-feeding clothing and supplies, cotton and wool organic baby clothing and bedding, wooden toys and furniture, a large assortment of diapers, and educational infant aids, call or log on to the Ecobaby website.

Ecobaby also has a baby shower registry where you can send in the names and addresses of thirty of your guests, together with your request list, and Ecobaby will send a catalog to each guest with your special requests. This offer is available to residents of the United States and Canada.

❦ Elizabeth Lee Designs
In the United States, call 800-449-3350
www.elizabethlee.com

Elizabeth Lee offers a large assortment of sewing patterns, including patterns for your baby's nursery decor, diaper bag patterns, infant dress patterns, sweet little layette patterns, car seat and stroller cover patterns, and more. Also available is a great selection of patterns designed for the breast-feeding mom. Call for a free catalog. This offer is available to residents of the United States only.

❦ Graham Kracker
In the United States, call 800-489-2820
www.grahamkracker.com (click on "Order Catalog")

Call for a free catalog of custom bedding for baby and child. This offer is available to residents of the United States only.

❦ Heart Thoughts
In the United States, call 800-670-4224

Call to receive free birth announcement samples and a catalog. This offer is available to residents of the United States only.

✿ JCPenney

In the United States or Canada, call 800-JCP-GIFT

www.jcpenney.com/jcp/default.asp (click on "Catalogs," then "Maternity Collection" or "The Baby Book")

JCPenney's Maternity Collection catalog features maternity fashions for all seasons and occasions. JCPenney's Baby Book offers a selection of nursery furniture, car seats, strollers, and more. Call or visit the website to request a free catalog. This offer is available to residents of the United States and Canada.

✿ JOCUS Educational Toys

In Canada, call 800-361-4587 (ext. 9496)

Jocus, a Canadian company established in 1978, offers wonderful, affordable toys, games, puzzles, and crafts for every stage of child development, as well as an extensive line of role-play costumes and multicultural puppets and dolls. They are the exclusive distributor of the Veritech independent math and language program for ages three to twelve. To receive a free catalog, earn free toys as a hostess, or find out how to become a Jocus Representative, call the toll-free number listed, or send an E-mail to mvandelinde@yahoo.com for more information. This offer is available to residents of Canada only.

✿ Kidalog

In the United States or Canada, call 780-672-1763 (sorry, not a toll-free number)

www.kidalog.com (click on "Request a Catalogue")

Kidalog (formerly Baby Love Products) offers thousands of baby, child, and mother care products. Call or visit the website to request a free catalog. This offer is available to residents of the United States and Canada.

❧ Lands' End Inc.

In the United States or Canada, call 800-356-4444

www.landsend.com (click on "Kids'," then "Latest Kids' Catalog")

Lands' End offers an assortment of adorable baby outfits, diaper bags, swimwear, bedding, blankets, and more. To receive the latest kids' catalog, call or request one online. This offer is available to residents of the United States and Canada.

❧ Little Me

In the United States, call 800-533-5437

Call to receive a free baby wear brochure of adorable swimsuits and dresses, sleepwear and playwear for newborns and infants, preemie clothing, gift sets, bath sets, and more. This offer is available to residents of the United States only.

❧ Little Tikes

In the United States or Canada, call 888-832-3203

www.littletikes.com (click on "Customer Service," then "Free Catalog")

Call to receive a free color catalog showcasing some of the newest "toys that last" from Little Tikes. You can also request a catalog at the website. This offer is available to residents of the United States and Canada.

❧ Mia Bambini and Company

www.miabambini.com

This cute website offers an assortment of baby clothing, including dresses and skirts, swimwear, tops, bottoms, footwear, and diaper products. Click on "Register Now" to receive the latest catalog via E-mail. This offer is available to residents of the United States and Canada.

❦ Motherhood Maternity

In the United States or Canada, call 800-4MOM2BE
www.motherhood.com

Call to receive a free maternity product catalog. This offer is available to residents of the United States and Canada.

❦ Motherwear

In the United States or Canada, call 800-950-2500
www.motherwear.com

Call or visit the website to request a free copy of Motherwear's color catalog featuring a full line of nursing clothing, nursing bras, breast-feeding products, pumps, accessories, and more. This catalog also contains a detailed sizing guide to help you select a nursing bra in the right size. The Motherwear website presents current and up-to-date breast-feeding information, as well as a breast-feeding booklet titled *Essential Breastfeeding Guide*, which you can download. This offer is available to residents of the United States and Canada.

❦ Mustela

In the United States, call 800-422-2987
www.mustelausa.com

Mustela has been taking care of babies since 1950. They offer hypoallergenic products, formulated for the delicate skin of newborns, as well as maternity skin-care products for expectant mothers. Call to receive a free product brochure, or visit the website to sign up for Mustela's free newsletter or to enter their online sweepstakes. This offer is available to residents of the United States only.

❧ Natural Baby

www.store.yahoo.com/naturalbaby/index.htm (click on "Catalog Request")

Each of the items at Natural Baby is made solely from things of this earth and is environmentally safe, organic, and natural. Natural Baby offers an assortment of baby items, including blankets and bedding, toys, clothing, and diapers, as well as herbal medicines, homeopathic remedies, and skin care products. Visit the Natural Baby website to request a free catalog. This offer is available to residents of the United States only.

❧ New Beginnings

In the United States or Canada, call 800-573-2049
www.yournewbeginnings.com

Call to receive a free New Beginnings birth announcement brochure and product samples. This offer is available to residents of the United States and Canada.

❧ One Step Ahead

In the United States or Canada, call 800-274-8440
www.onestepahead.com (click on "Request a Catalog")

Call to receive a free catalog offering a great selection of baby products, including strollers, carriers, car seats, and more. You can also request a catalog online. This offer is available to residents of the United States and Canada.

❧ Organic Bébé

In the United States, call 866-734-2634
www.organicbebe.com

Organic Bébé offers tons of natural products for babies, children, and mothers, including Baby's Only Organic Formula, Earth's Best Organic

Baby Food, organic bedding and clothing, natural skin care items, cloth diapers, and more. Call or go online for a free catalog of products. This offer is available to residents of the United States only.

✿ Peg-Pérego
In the United States, call 800-671-1701
In Canada, call 800-953-4488

The Peg-Pérego catalog offers a great assortment of infant car seats, high chairs, strollers, ride-on vehicles, and more. Call to receive a free catalog and list of dealers. Residents of the United States can order a free Peg-Pérego juvenile catalog and toy catalog online at www.pegperego.com. Canadian residents can order a free catalog online at www.pegperego.on.ca.

✿ Perfectly Safe
In the United States, call 800-837-5437
www.perfectlysafe.com (click on "Request Catalog")

Dedicated to child safety, the Perfectly Safe catalog offers child-proofing products for the entire home, your car, and travel. To receive a free catalog, call or visit the website. This offer is available to residents of the United States only.

✿ The Playstore
In the United States, call 877-876-1111
www.playstoretoys.com

Call for a free product catalog featuring quality wooden and natural toys, dress-up costumes, music and art supplies, games, dolls and puppets, playhouses, and more. This offer is available to residents of the United States only.

✿ Pride and Joy Announcements
In the United States or Canada, call 800-657-6404

Pride and Joy offers custom printed birth announcements and thank-you cards. Call to request a free Pride and Joy birth announcement catalog and samples. This offer is available to residents of the United States and Canada.

❦ The Right Start
In the United States or Canada, call 800-Little1
www.rightstart.com

The Right Start catalog offers products for mothers, infants, and children, including furniture, developmental toys, books, safety devices, music, videos, high chairs, and strollers. Call to order a free catalog. You can also register for the Right Start's baby registry online or by visiting a Right Start store location. This offer is available to residents of the United States and Canada.

❦ Safe Beginnings
In the United States or Canada, call 800-598-8911
www.safebeginnings.com (click on "Request Our Catalog")

Call or visit the website to request a free catalog of safety products and infant or toddler accessories.

❦ Stork Avenue
In the United States, call 800-861-5437
www.storkavenue.com (click on "Catalog Request")

Stork Avenue is one of the nation's premiere internet and catalog providers of birth announcements and invitations. Residents of the United States can call or visit the website to request a free catalog and card samples. Residents of Canada can request a free catalog and card samples online.

6

Web Resources for Parents

The World Wide Web is a fantastic resource for parents. Where else can you chat with other new parents from around the world with a click of the mouse, get up-to-date on the latest parenting information—even find out what to do when your child gets a carrot stuck up her nose!

The websites that I have listed in this chapter are exceptional and offer something of great interest to new or expecting Web-friendly parents. You will definitely want to bookmark these.

You could easily spend several hours on these websites, chatting with other new parents, participating in discussion boards, browsing through tons of parenting articles, hooking up with other moms and dads in your own area, getting support and advice or the latest medical, first-aid, and child safety information—you name it. There are even games, quizzes, and activities just for parents to keep you entertained for hours.

General Parenting Resources

The following websites contain general parenting information, including how to care for your baby, articles and information on breast-feeding, current information on all areas of pregnancy and childbirth, and more.

❦ Babies Today

www.babiestoday.com

The Babies Today website includes discussion boards, Q&As with experts, and tips on lifestyle issues like maternity fashion and finance management.

❦ Baby Bag

www.babybag.com

This parenting website features lots of pregnancy and childbirth stories, articles, product recalls, and parenting information.

❦ Canadian Childcare Directory

www.childcaredirectory.com

The Canadian Childcare Directory is a fun and easy-to-use directory that includes more than eight thousand listings for both parents and child care providers. You can search the interactive, user-friendly directory by entering your province, your city, and the first three digits of your postal code to find child care and educational facilities in your area. This is a Canadian service that is available free of charge, 24/7.

❦ Canadian Parents Online

www.canadianparents.com

At Canadian Parents Online you'll find numerous parenting articles, a free newsletter, a moms club, nutritious recipes, as well as access to a panel of experts, including pediatricians, dieticians, childbirth educators, and more.

❧ FamilyFun
www.family.com

This creative Disney site features activities and crafts, parenting articles, expert advice, thousands of family ideas and activities, games and recipes, and more. There is tons of stuff for moms, dads, and kids of all ages.

❧ Fisher-Price
www.fisher-price.com/us/myfp

The Fisher-Price website offers the *Grow-with-Me Parenting Guide* with information about your child's development, as well as help in finding the right toy or activity to stimulate your child. This guide covers the first month to the fifth year of a child's life and beyond.

❧ I Am Your Child Foundation
www.iamyourchild.org

Rob Reiner's I Am Your Child Foundation is a national public awareness campaign to make early childhood development a top national priority. One of the goals of this foundation is to try to influence public policy makers to increase spending on early childhood programs.

❧ Johnson's Baby
www.johnsonsbaby.com/stepbystep.asp

This Johnson & Johnson's website offers tons of printable step-by-step guides and excellent how-to videos you can view online to learn how to care for your new baby. The topics covered in these guides and instructional videos are as follows: "Bathing Your Baby"; "Breastfeeding Your Baby"; "Holding Your Baby, Dressing Your Baby, and More"; "Caring for Your Baby's Skin"; "Massage Your Baby"; and "Bonding with Your Baby."

❧ Lamaze International

> In the United States or Canada, call 800-368-4404
> www.lamaze-childbirth.com (click on "Especially for Expectant
> Parents")

"The mission of Lamaze International is to promote, support and protect normal birth through education and advocacy." The Lamaze website provides information on selecting a childbirth education class, tips for a healthy pregnancy, and pregnancy-related articles. If you are an expectant parent looking for a Lamaze childbirth education class, use the online Locator Service or call and ask to speak with a representative.

❧ National Adoption Foundation

> www.nafadopt.org

The National Adoption Foundation is a national organization that provides financial support and information and services for adoptive families before, during, and after their adoptions are finalized. The foundation also offers grants and loans to help families finance adoption.

❧ National Parenting Center

> www.tnpc.com

The National Parenting Center provides parents with responsible guidance from the world's most renowned child-rearing authorities. The organization also offers product reviews, children's craft ideas, and more.

❧ Parenthood.com

> www.parenthoodweb.com

This excellent all-purpose parenting site covers all areas of parenting and childbirth. You'll find a list of baby names, an ovulation calculator, a due date calculator, and more.

❧ Parenting.com

www.parenting.com/parenting/family_finance/index.html

If you're wondering how much it will actually cost you to have a baby, furnish his room, and keep him in diapers, check out this website, which will help you calculate your baby's and family's expenses. Also included is a basic budget sheet to help you figure out where and how you're spending your money.

❧ Parents Canada

www.parentscanada.com

This is an online community for new or expectant parents, from the publishers of *Parents Canada*, *Expecting*, and *Best Wishes* magazines. Expectant parents can visit PregnancyInc for the latest pregnancy-related information, including a pregnancy encyclopedia, a baby name finder, and more. New parents can visit BabyCare Online, which features a parenting guide with topics relating to newborns and children up to 2½ years of age. Leading health and medical authorities in Canada supply all the information on this website.

❧ Parents' Choice

www.parents-choice.org

Parents' Choice offers hundreds of online reviews and resources for parents and others who are involved in the lives of children. You will find information about children's toys, as well as help in making informed decisions about which products are right for your children.

❧ Parents.com

www.parents.com

This excellent parenting website contains tons of information for new or expecting moms, covering foods that are off-limits during pregnancy, false labor, dangerous herbs and medications, exercising safely

during pregnancy, and pregnancy first aid. Also available are free newsletters and articles, as well as age-by-age advice on every stage as your
child grows.

❦ Parents Helping Parents: The Parent-Directed Family Resource Center for Children with Special Needs
www.php.com

This parent-directed family resource center is available for parents
of children with physical, emotional, mental, or learning disabilities. It
is run for and by parents of children with special needs. The online
library provides tons of resources for special needs children.

❦ Parent Soup
www.parentsoup.com

One of the best parenting sites around, Parent Soup deals with
issues relating to children of all ages. The site offers a developmental
tracker, discussion boards, parenting workshops for women, articles
written by pediatric experts, chats, message boards, quizzes, and more.

❦ ParentsPlace.com
www.parentsplace.com

This website is a good starting point to find out current information on all areas of pregnancy and childbirth, as well as parenting of all
ages and stages. At this site you can also find bulletin boards and chats,
advice from the experts, pregnancy and due-date calendars, baby name
finders, and more.

❦ Parentstages.com
www.parentstages.com

Powered by Huggies, Parentstages.com offers tools to help you create a personalized birth plan, search for the perfect baby name, and fol-

low the daily development of your baby from conception to birth. You can also get advice on childproofing every corner of your home and read articles on numerous other parenting topics.

❦ Pregnancy by the Numbers Checklists

At these Parents.com websites for the expecting mom, you can print out a first, second, or third trimester to-do list, a handy reminder list of the things you will want to do throughout the different stages of your pregnancy.

First Trimester To-Do List:
www.parents.com/articles/pregnancy/1133.jsp
Second Trimester To-Do List:
www.parents.com/articles/pregnancy/1134.jsp
Third Trimester To-Do List:
www.parents.com/articles/pregnancy/1135.jsp

❦ Today's Parent
www.todaysparent.com

The Today's Parent website provides free contests, quizzes, craft ideas, recipes for kids, book reviews, forums, features, and details on upcoming special events. You can create a digital family photo album to share photos of your family with others. Click on "Parenting A-Z" to access the Today's Parent Library, where you can find tons of articles based on the age of your child, birth and pregnancy-related articles, and more.

❦ Zero to Three
www.zerotothree.org

Zero to Three is a nonprofit organization whose goal is to promote healthy development of infants and toddlers from birth to age 3. It is the nation's leading resource on the first three years of life. The website offers great resources for parents, including parenting tips, articles, information on early literacy, and more. At www.zerotothree.org/ brainwonders you can learn some fascinating facts about how the brain develops from conception to 3 years of age.

Health and Medical Resources

As each situation is unique, the medical information provided in these websites should not be used as a substitute for the medical care and personal attention of your physician or for any emergency situations. There may be variations in treatment that your physician may recommend based on individual facts and circumstances. The information in these websites is available solely to educate you and arm you with the types of questions you will need to ask your doctor in an attempt to better prepare you for your next doctor's visit.

❧ American Academy of Pediatrics
www.aap.org

The American Academy of Pediatrics is dedicated to the health, safety, and well-being of infants, children, adolescents, and young adults. The organization's website offers a wealth of information on such topics as child health and nutrition, immunizations, children with disabilities, and everything you need to know to keep your child healthy.

❧ American Dental Association
www.ada.org/public/media/psa/index.html

The American Dental Association offers thirty-second videotaped or animated messages to help teach your little one to start brushing her teeth. These cute online minivideos include "Baby Digby's First Tooth," "Baby Bottle Tooth Decay," "Healthy Snacks with Dudley," "Dudley's Dental Quiz," and more. Great for when baby's first teeth start to appear!

❦ Canadian Paediatric Society
www.caringforkids.cps.ca

Caring For Kids is a Canadian website developed by the Canadian Paediatric Society. This site was designed to provide parents with information about their children's health and well-being. All information provided at this website is reviewed by a committee of experts. Topics covered include "Pregnancy and Babies," "When Your Child Is Sick," "Healthy Eating," "Immunization," "Keeping Your Child Healthy," and more.

❦ Children's Tylenol and Children's Motrin Dosing Charts
www.getwellkids.com (click on "Dosing Charts")

Visit the website for a printable dosing chart for Children's Tylenol and Children's Motrin, arranged according to a child's weight and age, to be sure you give your child the right dose every time.

❦ Complete Home Medical Guide
http://cpmcnet.columbia.edu/texts/guide

This website from the Columbia University College of Physicians and Surgeons features a great section on how to get the most out of your health care system. It also provides helpful information on what to do about many child-related medical emergencies, health issues and illnesses, and more.

❦ KidsHealth
www.kidshealth.org

The KidsHealth website is a great site for parents who have questions about their kids' illnesses. It also contains tons of articles on pregnancy and childbirth.

❦ March of Dimes
www.modimes.org

For more than sixty-four years, the March of Dimes, through its programs and research, has saved millions of babies from death or disability. In addition, the organization helps moms and babies get access to health care. The website contains valuable information for new or expecting parents on infant health, birth defects, the importance of folic acid, premature births, and the importance of prenatal care, as well as numerous other articles on pregnancy and parenting.

✺ Mayo Clinic

www.mayoclinic.com (click on "Condition Centers," then
"Children's Conditions")

Tap into the expertise of one of the world's most renowned medical research institutions, the Mayo Clinic, to find valuable medical information on common problems of children and on pediatric conditions, as well as medical quizzes. Topics range from ear infections to broken bones. The "Pregnancy and Reproduction" section offers moms great information on numerous topics, including labor, delivery, newborn care, and pregnancy complications.

✺ *The Merck Manual of Medical Information—Home Edition*

www.merckhomeedition.com/home.html

The Merck Manual, written by nearly two hundred leading medical experts, is a best-selling medical reference that has sold more than two million copies worldwide. It contains complete and in-depth medical information about diseases, diagnosis, prevention and treatment, and more. Visit the website to view the interactive version or the text-based version, both available free of charge and written in easy-to-understand English. A great page to bookmark!

✺ Postpartum Stress Center

www.postpartumstress.com

The Postpartum Stress Center specializes in the treatment of postpartum illnesses. The website offers information on postpartum depression. It offers self-help suggestions on things that can make you feel better, as well as information on where you can go to get help, support groups, grief counseling, and more.

✿ Postpartum Support International
www.chss.iup.edu/postpartum

Postpartum Support International provides social support and information regarding postpartum mood disorders and depression. The website offers postpartum chat rooms and bulletin boards. There are online self-assessment surveys for moms who are depressed or stressed, as well as information about anxiety and panic attacks, postpartum fatigue, exhaustion, and more.

✿ UnitedHealth Foundation
www.unitedhealthfoundation.org

This website provides information on becoming more knowledgeable about your own health and your health care options, as well as information on how to be a smarter health care consumer.

Child Safety and First Aid

Every parent should visit and bookmark the websites in this section to familiarize themselves with first-aid procedures, the basics of infant and child CPR, and what to do in case of an emergency. What you learn at these sites may save your child's life!

✿ Band-Aid
www.bandaid.com/first_aid_guide.html

At the Band-Aid website you can download a free printable *First Aid Guide* with basic emergency information on tons of first-aid topics, including shock, frostbite, sunburn, chemical burns, unconsciousness, and more.

❧ **Canadian Consumer Information Gateway**
www.consumerinformation.ca (click on "Safety")

This site provides a vast amount of reliable safety information from Government of Canada departments and agencies. Topics covered include food safety, household safety, medication, product safety and recalls, and more.

❧ **Clue in to Safety**
www.clueintosafety.com

Clue in to Safety is a safety project brought to you by Ford, in cooperation with Blue's Clues, to help parents and children learn important safety lessons. Click on "Visit the Front Seat for Parents!" for valuable information on vehicle safety, home safety, fire safety, water safety, and police safety. This website also offers children's safety games, printable coloring pages, and a free poster.

❧ **Complete Home Medical Guide**
http://cpmcnet.columbia.edu/texts/guide

See the "First Aid and Safety" section at this excellent medical website (from the Columbia University College of Physicians and Surgeons) to learn the basics of CPR and life support, including CPR on infants and children, as well as basic first-aid procedures.

❧ **DaimlerChrysler SeatCheck**
In the United States, call 866-SEAT-CHECK
www.seatcheck.org

At this website you can search for a listing of child passenger safety seat inspection locations nationwide, where inspectors can provide guidance on proper child restraint use and installation. Visit the website or call to find an inspection location near you. This program is available to residents of the United States only.

❧ Enfamil Safety Tips
www.enfamil.com/safetytips.html

This informative website will provide you with safety tips on the following topics: car seats, choking, crying baby, poisoning, SIDS, sun care, wounds and burns, and more.

❧ Juvenile Products Manufacturers Association
www.jpma.org

This website informs consumers about the safe use of juvenile products and industry issues. Information is available to help parents in selecting safe juvenile products for their children. During your visit to the website, make sure you check out the "Baby Safety" section, which presents valuable information on providing a safe environment for your baby in the kitchen, bedroom, living room, carport, and bath.

❧ KidsHealth
http://www.kidshealth.org/parent/firstaid_safe/index.html

This website covers tons of first-aid topics, including emergencies, home safety and first aid, safety away from the home, and outdoors and seasonal safety.

❧ Parents.com
www.parents.com

This website is an excellent resource for first-aid and safety instructions. All new or expecting parents should visit this website to become familiar with what to do in case of an emergency. Some of the topics covered include what to do if your child is choking, what foods can cause choking in young children, how to tell if your child's case is urgent, when to call 911, baby safety basics, and more. The following informative articles can be viewed online:

- "Baby Safety Basics": www.parents.com/articles/health/2037.jsp. This article covers such important topics as bathtub safety and drowning, choking, falls, car seat mistakes, and more.

- "Burn Danger Checklist": www.parents.com/articles/health/2084.jsp. Take these simple steps throughout the house to protect your child from burn-related injuries.

- "Checklist: 10 First-Aid Must-Haves (for Cuts)": www.parents.com/articles/health/2102.jsp. This is a handy checklist of the ten emergency essentials to have readily available to treat your child's cuts and scrapes.

- "Checklist: Top Food Hazards": www.parents.com/articles/health/2099.jsp. This is a listing of foods to avoid giving your child since they may cause choking.

- "Fire Prevention Checklist": www.parents.com/articles/health/2090.jsp. Provided are precautions that you can take throughout your house to reduce the risk of fire.

- "First Aid for Burns and Scalds": www.parents.com/articles/health/2059.jsp. Kids under the age of 5 are at greater risk for burns because they don't understand the consequences of fire and heat. This section covers first-, second-, and third-degree burns and what you can do to save your child's skin.

- "First Aid for Choking": www.parents.com/articles/health/2060.jsp. Provided are life-saving tips, including what to do in an emergency, how to save a choking child under 1 year of age, and how to save an older child who is choking.

- "First Aid for Cuts and Bleeding": www.parents.com/articles/health/2061.jsp. Check out this website for instructions on treating your child's cuts, bruises, and bleeding.

- "First-Aid Kit Essentials": www.parents.com/articles/health/2052.jsp. Included is a handy checklist of first-aid kit essentials to keep in your at-home first-aid kit.

- "First Aid on Vacation": www.parents.com/articles/health/2126.jsp. This article discusses how to prevent injuries and treat illnesses when away from home on vacation.

- "Over-the-Counter Medication Guide": www.parents.com/articles/health/2064.jsp. Don't give your child the wrong dose of a common medicine. Check out this guide for proper dosage instructions.

- "Strangulation and Suffocation": www.parents.com/articles/health/2065.jsp. This article explains what to do to prevent strangulation and suffocation and what to do in case of emergency.

- "Treating Baby Bites": www.parents.com/articles/health/2080.jsp. Information is provided on what to do if another child bites your little one.

- "When to Call 911": www.parents.com/articles/health/2036.jsp. This article offers information on how you can tell if your child's case is urgent and when you should call 911.

Safe Kids
www.safekids.org

The National Safe Kids Campaign is dedicated to preventing the number one killer of children 14 and younger—unintentional injury. At the Safe Kids website, you'll find more than five hundred ways to keep your children safe, including information on how to safely wear a bike helmet, how to properly install a child car seat, and more. To learn more about this campaign and how to keep your children safe, visit the website.

Safe Kids Canada
www.safekidscanada.ca (click on "Safety Tips to Keep Kids Safe")

Safe Kids Canada is a terrific website that offers tons of ways to help keep kids safe. Topics covered include safety tips for children under the age of 5, airline travel safety, water safety, winter safety, first-aid instructions, and more. The website also offers a home safety, road safety, and playground safety checklist.

❧ U.S. Consumer Product Safety Commission
www.cpsc.gov

The goal of the U.S. Consumer Product Safety Commission is to help keep families safe by reducing the risk of death or injury from consumer products. This website provides you with a list of products that have been recalled, and it reports unsafe products as well.

Resources for Parents of Multiples

Being a parent of multiples brings about unique challenges and experiences, beginning with the pregnancy of multiples as well as the labor and delivery, then on to coordinating nursing, feeding, and sleeping schedules—and trying to get your babies on the same schedules. The following websites offer articles, tips, and support groups, as well as advice from other parents of multiples.

❧ National Organization of Mothers of Twins Club
www.nomotc.org

NOMOTC promotes the special aspects of child development that relate to multiple birth children. The website will connect you to local twin and multiples clubs.

❧ Parents of Multiples Across Canada
www.mom2many.com

This Internet community for Canadian parents of multiples offers forums, resources, birth stories, chats, articles, and more.

❧ Twins
www.twinsmagazine.com

The *Twins* magazine website provides great resources for parents of twins and multiples, including information on nursing and feeding your multiples, message boards, and tons of other great resources.

❧ Twinstuff.Com
www.twinstuff.com

This large Web community for twins, triplets, and higher, as well as their families, contains a message board where you can view and post messages, links for shopping for multiples, and other pertinent information regarding raising multiples.

❧ Twinsworld.com
www.twinsworld.com

This website features twin festival information, twin merchandise, bulletin boards, chats, and jokes for parents of multiples, as well as links to other multiples' websites.

Preemie Parenting Resources

A quarter of a million babies are born prematurely every year in the United States alone. As premature infants will often need special care, I have listed the following websites that deal with the challenges and complications faced by parents with premature infants. These websites offer support groups, resources, and articles, as well as inspirational stories from parents of preemies.

❧ Baby Place
www.baby-place.com/premature.htm

This website contains tons of links to support groups, resources, and articles for parents of premature infants. You can find resources dealing with how to care for your premature baby, miracle birth stories, preemie chats, and more.

❦ Preemie Care and Development

www.babyparenting.about.com/library/weekly/aao510o1a.htm

About.com presents materials on preemie care and development for parents of preemies. You'll find support groups and other resources, as well as information about preterm labor and delivery, sleep apnea in children, complications of prematurity, preemie care, and other medical issues relating to infants who were born prematurely.

❦ Preemie Page

www.motherstuff.com/html/preemie.htm

Parents of preemies will find links to interesting articles, preemie health information, support groups, and other Internet resources at this website.

❦ Preemie Parenting

www.preemieparenting.com

Preemie Parenting is a place created for parents and loved ones of premature infants, as well as for women experiencing a high-risk or complicated pregnancy. The site offers access to information, support, and resources. You can read preemie birth stories and inspirational pieces, and you can learn about infant medical complications, problems, and special needs, as well as about medical causes of prematurity. Also provided is a list of parenting support groups.

For Moms

The following resources are available for all kinds of moms: single moms, stay-at-home moms, and working moms.

Speaking of stay-at-home and working moms, at this point in the book I just thought I'd take some time out to vent a bit—hope you don't mind! Stay-at-home moms, working moms—we're all moms, doing our best to raise our children. I've been both a stay-at-home mom as well as a working mom. My children never stopped loving me when I decided to go back to work. In fact, our relationship was just as close as ever and never suffered in the least.

I guess I'm getting a little tired of people who judge you as a parent because you decide to work outside of the home or choose to stay at home with your children. The most important thing is the quality time that you do spend with your children when you're with them, and that you give them all the love, support, and encouragement they need.

So let's stop wasting our time judging each other and concentrate on the things in life that are a true concern—the children who really do need special help and attention, such as children who are abused, neglected, or homeless. Okay, moving right along. . . .

BlueSuitMom.com
www.bluesuitmom.com

This website for working moms offers practical tips on balancing work and home. You'll find tips for planning meals, travel, and managing time, as well as information on working from home, women-owned businesses, and ways to find time for the family. Ideas for family activities are also provided.

FitMommies.com
www.fitmommies.com

For the active mom, this website features workouts and exercises for all levels of fitness, activities and information for active families, nutrition information, healthy recipes, and more.

National Organization of Single Mothers
www.singlemothers.org

According to this organization, "Today, 13 million single mothers are raising America's children. In fact, single parents make up the majority of households." This website provides a great support system for single moms, helping single mothers get in touch with other single moms and offering help and advice for successfully raising your children. Single mothers can find articles, tips, and advice to help them deal with the day-to-day challenges of single parenting.

❦ National Women's Health Information Center
www.4women.gov

The National Women's Health Information Center offers information on a wide variety of women's health-related issues, including pregnancy, postpartum depression, breast cancer, breast-feeding, nutrition, contraception and gynecology, abuse, and general women's health concerns.

❦ SingleRose.com
www.singlerose.com

SingleRose.com is for single mothers who are raising their children alone. The site offers discussion boards, chats, and articles on single parenting. Some of the topics covered at this site include divorce recovery, dealing with anger, child support, and custody issues.

❦ Stay at Home Mom
www.stayathomemom.com

The Stay at Home Mom website was designed to create a positive place for stay-at-home moms to gather and encourage each other. The forum-driven website contains a message board where you can read and post messages, read articles, and more.

For Dads

For the Web-friendly dads who want to connect with other dads, obtain up-to-date parenting information, sharpen their cooking skills, read articles, and get advice from other fathers, these terrific fathering websites are for you! They suggest all kinds of activities you can do together with your kids, offer help and advice for the stay-at-home dad, feature father-friendly chats, and more.

❦ Center for Successful Fathering
www.fathering.org

This website has a self-assessment test for dads, as well as numerous links to other fathering websites. Information is available to provide dads with skills and resources to assist them in becoming the best dads they can be!

❦ Fathers Network
www.fathersnetwork.org

This website presents a wealth of resources and information for fathers, including father support groups, organizations, and more. The mission of the Fathers Network is to support fathers and families who are raising children with special needs and developmental disabilities.

❦ Father's World
www.fathersworld.com

Dads will have access here to resources pertaining to many areas of interest, such as support and parenting education, health, recipes, news, legal issues, and more. The goal of Father's World is to connect fathers with each other and with various support agencies and associations.

❦ National Center for Fathering
www.fathers.com

This fathering website provides practical "how-to" oriented resources to prepare dads for nearly every fathering situation. It is a great resource for dads seeking to strengthen their fathering skills. Fathers can sign up at the National Center for Fathering to receive *Fathers.Com Weekly*, a free weekly newsletter delivered via E-mail.

✿ Parenthub

www.parenthub.com/parenting/father.htm

This website contains links to magazines, articles, and resources for single dads, stepdads, and divorced dads. Dads will have access to discipline tips for single dads, studies of children in fatherless homes, and advice from other fathers.

✿ Slowlane.com

www.slowlane.com

Slowlane.com offers stay-at-home dads a wide variety of online references, resources, and links to other fathering sites. The website provides dads with a searchable collection of articles and media clips written by, for, and about primary caregiving fathers.

Free Online Medical Advice

At the following medical websites, highly respected doctors, pediatricians, and other medical experts are available to answer your medical and parenting questions. Just type in your question at the website, and these professionals will do their best to answer you in a timely fashion.

These websites offer a wealth of free medical advice and information for parents, as well as a chance to view tons of medical-related articles. Topics covered include pregnancy, labor and birth, newborn issues, pregnancy complications, prenatal health, nutrition, breast-feeding, children's health, growth and development, pediatric illnesses, and more.

Please note: These online doctors and medical experts will try their very best to answer all of your medical questions. But because many of these medical websites receive hundreds, even thousands, of questions each week, they may not always be able to answer each and every question individually. For these reasons, many of the websites have posted online Q&As in different medical categories, which you can view to look for an answer to your question. You may want to check out these posted Q&As first before you ask the doctor a question.

As each situation is unique, the medical information provided in these websites should not be used as a substitute for the medical care and personal attention of your physician or for any emergency situations. There may be variations in treatment that your physician may recommend based on individual facts and circumstances. The information in these websites is available solely to educate you and arm you with the types of questions you will need to ask your doctor in an attempt to better prepare you for your next doctor's visit.

AllExperts.com
www.allexperts.com

AllExperts.com, the oldest and largest free Q&A service on the Internet, has thousands of volunteer experts available to answer your questions. Just pick a category, click, and ask a question. Categories include everything from arts and humanities to television and radio. There are too many topics to list! The "parenting/family" category covers such areas as adoption, day care, pregnancy and birth, fatherhood, grandparenting, single parents, stay-at-home parents, children's books, parenting special needs children, parenting multiples, parenting babies and toddlers, and more.

Answers from Mayo Clinic
www.mayoclinic.com/findinformation/answers/index.cfm

Specialists from the Mayo Clinic will answer your medical questions in a wide range of categories, including food and nutrition, mental health, pregnancy and reproduction, women's health, children's conditions, and other pregnancy-related concerns. As these specialists receive thousands of questions each week, they cannot answer all of them, but you can view their posted Q&As online in the many different categories as listed above.

Ask Dr. Sears

www.parenting.com/parenting/experts/sears/index.html

Dr. Sears is a leading pediatrician and the author of more than twenty-five books on child care. You can view his responses to new concerns every day on his special message board or ask him a question at the website.

Asking the Doc.com

www.askingthedoc.com

The doctors at this site will answer your medical questions and provide you with information about your health through confidential E-mail. These doctors take the time to explain medical issues in simple terms that you can understand.

Ask the Dietitian

www.dietitian.com/index.html

A registered dietitian is available to answer your nutrition questions in the following categories: infants and toddlers, food allergies, calories, eating habits, and more. The online dietitian will read your E-mail and try to answer your questions in a timely fashion.

Ask the Immunization Experts

www.immunize.org/catg.d/p2021.htm

At this website you can view immunization-related questions and answers concerning diphtheria, tetanus, pertussis, polio, measles, mumps, rubella, and others.

Ask the Pediatrician

www.keepkidshealthy.com/ask_the_pediatrician.html

At Keep Kids Healthy.com you can ask the pediatrician questions about your child's health, growth, and development, as well as about your child's symptoms and illnesses.

❀ **Ask the Pros**
www.childbirth.org/AskANurse/pros.html

At this medical website you can ask a childbirth educator questions about pregnancy, labor, and birth, ask a doula questions about the basics of pregnancy, birth, and breast-feeding, ask a lactation consultant questions about breast-feeding, ask a midwife questions about homebirth and midwifery, or ask a nurse questions about fertility and pregnancy.

❀ **Call Your Pediatrician**
www.callyourped.com

This website provides information on common illnesses and how they can be safely treated, as well as advice on when to call the doctor, home medical treatments, and more. Among the illnesses covered are asthma, chickenpox, coughs and colds, croup, diaper rash, dehydration, ear and eye infections, fever, and vomiting.

❀ **Child Behavioral Health Forum**
www.medhelp.org (click on "Child Behavior")

At this Med Help International forum, doctors from Harvard Vanguard Medical Associates will answer questions about child discipline, child behavior management, normal child development, and more.

❀ **Dr. Paul's Child Health and Wellness Info Site**
www.drpaul.com

Dr. Paul is a highly respected Canadian pediatrician. At this site, you can ask the doctor a question or search through tons of Dr. Paul's articles relating to different parenting topics, such as newborn issues, growth and development, nutrition, breast-feeding, and other child health and wellness issues.

❀ **DRs4Kids**
www.drs4kids.com/index.html

Pediatrician Dr. Fredric Suser is available online to share his twenty years of private practice experience with you. You can ask the doctor a question or search his website to get answers to medical topics concerning infants, children, and adolescents, explained in a way that is easy for parents to understand.

❦ Dr. Spock Company

www.drspock.com (click on "Ask Our Experts")

When you register online as a Dr. Spock user, you can submit a question, which will then be directed to the right expert. There are all kinds of experts available at this website who will answer as many questions as possible in categories such as pregnancy and birth, pediatric behavior and development, infectious diseases, and childhood immunizations.

❦ Earlychildhood.com

www.earlychildhood.com (click on "Ask Our Experts")

The specialists available at this website will deal with such issues as binkies, blankies, and bottles, potty training, bed-wetting, and other early childhood concerns.

❦ Pediatric Neurosurgery

www.nyneurosurgery.org/child/pediatric_index.htm

At this Institute for Neurology and Neurosurgery website, you can view topics relating to pediatric neurosurgery, including spina bifida and cerebral palsy, as well as ask the doctor a neurological question.

❦ Vascular Birthmarks Foundation

www.birthmark.org/ask_the_doctor.htm

Here you can ask the doctor a question about your child's birthmark, including hemangiomas, port wine stains, and other vascular malformations.

Free Government Resources for New or Expecting Parents

The government offers a wealth of free resources to new or expecting parents, including parenting publications and other literature, programs that offer free financial assistance and nutritional foods to parents, and various tax breaks and other benefits to help parents with the cost of raising a child.

Take the time to familiarize yourself with what is available from the government, as listed throughout this chapter.

Free Publications

The informative publications listed in this section are free and readily available to you as a parent. Simply call or go online to request those publications that are of interest to you.

Government of Canada Publications
In Canada, call 800-O-CANADA

Call the Government of Canada to request any of the following free publications. Calls are answered personally in the caller's choice of either English or French. Phone lines are open Monday to Friday, 8 A.M. to 8 P.M. EST. (Those who are hearing impaired can call the Government of Canada at 800-465-7735 to order these free publications.)

- *10 Valuable Tips for Successful Breastfeeding*. This informative pamphlet, aimed at new mothers, covers the basics of breast-feeding.

- *Back to Sleep*. SIDS is less common in babies who sleep on their backs. This pamphlet, which is also available at www.back-to-sleep.com, explains the correct sleeping positions for infants, as well as other important facts that you need to know to reduce the risk of SIDS and suffocation.

- *Canada's Food Guide to Healthy Eating*. This booklet offers practical guidelines you can use daily to make healthy food choices for you and your family.

- *The Child Health Record*. This pocket-sized booklet provides an easy way to keep track of important facts about your child's development, including health checkups, weight, immunization history, feedings, injuries and illnesses, and more.

- *International Adoption and the Immigration Process*. This booklet is designed to serve as a guide to the process of international adoption and the entry of adoptive children into Canada. It outlines the basic steps and procedures that must be followed.

- *Is Your Child Safe?* Injury is the leading cause of death among children and youth in Canada. Many of these injuries occur at home. This publication informs parents how they can make their environment safer for their children. It covers home safety, fire safety, emergency preparedness, and more.

- *Keep Kids Safe*. This publication discusses child safety, including the proper use of car seats, child restraint recalls, booster seats, and more.

❦ HRSA (Health Resources and Services Administration) Information Center
In the United States, call 888-AskHRSA
www.ask.hrsa.gov/search.cfm

The following publications are available free of charge from the HRSA Information Center of the U.S. Department of Health and Human Services. To order a free single copy of a publication, call or visit the website.

- *Bright Futures Family Pocket Guide: Raising Healthy Infants, Children, and Adolescents.* This guide is written especially for families to prepare them to become better partners for their children's health. It highlights important child health topics, including what will happen at a health visit from birth to age 21, how your child grows, and what to expect when your child gets older. Also featured are family websites, resources for families, tip sheets, and more. Order by Inventory Code Number MCHN022.

- *Bright Futures for Families: Lead Poisoning.* This booklet contains information on lead poisoning in children. It informs the public about lead poisoning, its causes, and its problems. The booklet will show you how you can protect your children from lead poisoning at home and at school. Order by Inventory Code Number MCHM067.

- *Healthy Foods, Healthy Baby.* This booklet provides the pregnant adolescent with nutrition guidelines and solutions to common complaints such as heartburn, constipation, and nausea. This booklet also includes lists of healthy foods, with great emphasis placed on the four basic food groups, as well as a chart promoting healthy weight gain. Order by Inventory Code Number MCHM001.

- *A Healthy Start: Begin Before Baby's Born.* This brochure provides helpful hints for a healthy pregnancy and a healthy baby in a question-and-answer format. Order by Inventory Code Number MCHN036.

- *Insure Kids Now* CD-ROM. This free compact disc offers information on where to call to obtain health insurance for infants, children, and teens. Order by Inventory Code Number HRS00114.

- *Newborn Screening: State Policy Directions and Trends.* This informative newsletter talks about the newborn screening laws enacted in the 1960s and 1970s and the advances in the area of genetic sciences. Order by Inventory Code Number MCHN069.

- *Newsweek: Your Child. Newsweek* magazine's fall edition provides valuable information on a child's growth and development from birth, all the way to three years of age. This special edition covers a child's learning stages, the health and emotions of children up to three years of age, and more. Order by Inventory Code Number MCHN008.

- *Paying the Bills: Tips for Families on Financing Health Care for Children with Special Needs.* This booklet includes tips in the following areas: getting started, making your child's health insurance work for your family, making public programs work for you, tackling medical bills, influencing decision-makers, documenting your child's special needs, cost savings, finding other sources of funding, and connecting with other families. Order by Inventory Code Number MCHL094.

- *Working and Breastfeeding: Can You Do It? Yes, You Can!* This booklet contains useful information for mothers who may be returning to work while they are still breast-feeding. It explains the benefits of breast-feeding, for mother and baby, and how to fit breast-feeding into a working mother's schedule. Order by Inventory Code Number MCHL007.

❧ National Adoption Information Clearinghouse
www.calib.com/naic/pubs/index.cfm

The National Adoption Information Clearinghouse is the nation's number one source of information about adoption. The clearinghouse offers a number of information packages and a ton of publications, too many to mention, on all areas of adoption. Log on to the website for a listing of free publications.

❧ National Center for Missing and Exploited Children
In the United States or Canada, call 800-843-5678
   (ask for booklet #12)
www.ncmec.org

Call to receive the free safety booklet *Just in Case . . . Parental Guidelines in Case You Need a Babysitter*, with safety tips, information on finding and hiring a baby-sitter, and more. You can also call if you have information on missing or exploited children. This offer is available to residents of the United States and Canada.

❧ National Center on Birth Defects and Developmental Disabilities
In the United States, call 888-232-5929

Call for a free booklet on folic acid and its role in preventing birth defects. This offer is available to residents of the United States only.

❧ U.S. Consumer Product Safety Commission
In the United States or Canada, call 800-638-2772
www.cpsc.gov/cpscpub/pubs/pub_idx.html

The following U.S. Consumer Product Safety Commission publications are available, free of charge, if you request them by calling or visiting the website.

- *Baby Product Safety Alert.* This publication discusses strangulation, suffocation, and other hazards in the use of cribs, crib toys, strollers, bunk beds, plastic bags, rattles, and more. Order CPSC Document #250.

- *Baby Safety Shower How-To Kit.* If you're looking for ways to help parents take better care of their children by giving them new ideas about keeping their babies safe at home, consider organizing a baby safety shower for yourself or for an expectant friend. A baby safety shower is a learning party where all the activities revolve around home safety themes. Everyone attending the shower will learn tips to keep their children safe. The U.S. Consumer Product Safety Commission and Gerber Products Company developed this baby safety shower initiative to help good parents become even better ones. The materials you'll need to get started are included in this kit. Also provided is a Baby Safety Checklist, which can be used as a growth chart to help you watch your baby grow. Order CPSC Document #207.

- *Child Care Safety Checklist for Parents and Child Care Providers.* Use the safety tips provided in this handy checklist to help keep your children safe. Topics include choosing a crib, safety gates, bedding, window blind and curtain cords, and more. Order CPSC Document #242.

- *Childproofing Your Home.* This booklet lists twelve safety devices to protect your children, including window guards, safety latches and locks, safety gates, outlet covers, and more. Order CPSC Document #202.

- *For Kids' Sake: Think Toy Safety.* This publication covers toy safety, as well as buying, maintaining, and storing infants' and children's toys. Order CPSC Document #281.

- *Tips for Your Baby's Safety.* This publication contains a Nursery Equipment Safety Checklist to help you when buying new or secondhand nursery equipment. It can also be used when checking over nursery equipment in your home or in other facilities that care for infants and young children. Order CPSC Document #200.

- *Which Toy for Which Child: Birth to 5 Years of Age.* This is a consumers' guide for selecting suitable toys for infants and children from birth to age 5. Order CPSC Document #285.

Free Financial Assistance, Tax Breaks, and Other Benefits in the United States

The government offers assistance to families with children in various ways, including financial assistance and support services for low-income families, health insurance programs, food and nutrition programs, as well as beneficial tax credits to those who are eligible. Please review the following listings for more information on these programs and services and their eligibility requirements.

❀ Adoption Credit

www.irs.gov/formspubs/ (type "Topic 607" in the search box)

To help offset the costs involved in adoption, adoptive parents can claim a tax credit for up to $10,000 for qualifying expenses paid to adopt a child. Qualifying expenses include adoption fees, court costs, legal fees, traveling, and other necessary expenses. Visit the website for more information on this benefit.

❀ Centers for Medicare and Medicaid Services

In the United States, call 410-786-3000 (sorry, not a toll-free number)

www.hcfa.gov/medicaid

Medicaid is a joint federal and state program that provides health insurance and medical assistance to approximately forty million low-income Americans. It is the single largest provider of family planning services to women of reproductive health age. Nationwide, about 40 percent of all births are funded by Medicaid, as many pregnant women can qualify for it even if their income is greater than the federal poverty level. Without the Medicaid program, millions of women and their children would be left with no health insurance at all. The Medicaid program varies considerably from state to state, as each state establishes its own eligibility standards and administers its own program. At http://cms.hhs.gov/medicaid/mcontact.asp you will find state Medicaid contacts, as well as state-by-state toll-free numbers where you can contact your state officials for details about the Medicaid program in your state. For more information about Medicaid eligibility, Medicaid services, and how to apply for Medicaid, go online or call the Centers for Medicare and Medicaid Services. For a listing of phone numbers of local Medicaid offices, you can also call 800-633-4227.

❦ Child Care Tax Credit

> www.irs.gov (type "Child and Dependent Care Expenses" in the
>   search box)

You may be able to claim a tax credit if you are using child care or a child care program for your baby while you are working. Visit the website for further details and eligibility requirements, as well as to download the required forms necessary to apply for this benefit.

❦ The Child Tax Credit (CTC)

> www.irs.gov/formspubs/ (type "Child Tax Credit Forms" in the
>   search box)

Uncle Sam grants a tax credit to eligible families for each child under the age of 17. Over the next eight years, the credit will be increased from $600 to $1,000 per child by tax year 2010. The CTC is partially refundable for families with yearly earnings over $10,000. Visit the website for more information, as well as to download the CTC forms.

❦ Child Welfare League of America

> In the United States, call 202-638-2952 (sorry, not a
>   toll-free number)
> www.cwla.org

The Child Welfare League of America assists more than 3.5 million abused and neglected children and their families each year. The organization offers families a wide range of services. For more information on the services available, call or check out the website for details.

❀ Early Head Start National Resource Center

U.S. Department of Health and Human Services

Head Start Bureau

330 C Street SW

Washington, DC 20202

In the United States, call 866-763-6481

www.ehsnrc.org

Early Head Start, a program for low-income families, provides services to low-income pregnant women, as well as families with infants and toddlers. This community-based program is designed to enhance children's physical, social, emotional, and intellectual development. It offers health, mental health, and family support services, including services to women before, during, and after pregnancy; information on nutrition; child care services; parenting education; and more. This program also supports parents by helping them move toward economic independence through various educational services. To find out if you are eligible to participate in this program, log on to the website or submit your questions about Early Head Start to the address listed above. This program is available to residents of the United States.

❀ Family and Medical Leave

In the United States, call 866-487-9243

www.dol.gov (U.S. Department of Labor)

www.nationalpartnership.org (click on "Work and Family")

The Family and Medical Leave Act (FMLA), issued by the U.S. Department of Labor, is designed to help working people fulfill both their work and family responsibilities. This act allows families to take unpaid time off to care for their loved ones (such as caring for a new baby or newly adopted child or a sick parent, spouse, or child) or to recover from their own serious illnesses, without putting their jobs at risk. The FMLA covers any pregnancy-related leave that is medically necessary, including childbirth and recovery. Both you and your husband can each take up to twelve weeks' leave when the baby comes. You must have worked for your employer for at least twelve months, and for a minimum of 1,250 hours during the last year, and you must work for a company with more than fifty employees to be eligible to take up to twelve weeks of unpaid leave a year that is job secured. You can download a free copy of the *Guide to the Family and Medical Leave Act: Questions and Answers*, which will give you current information on the act, as well as eligibility requirements. You can order a free hard copy of this publication by sending an E-mail to info@nationalpartnership.org. Please put "FMLA Guide–English" in the subject line, and be sure to include your name, your mailing address, and the number of copies needed in the message. For questions about the FMLA, contact the U.S. Department of Labor's Wage and Hour Division at the toll-free number listed above, or contact your state labor department or your union.

Federal Information Center
In the United States, call 800-FED-INFO

The National Call Center will answer your questions about federal agencies, programs, benefits, and services. Frequently requested information is given in recordings available through an automated service.

Food Stamp Program
In the United States, call 800-221-5689 (USDA Food Stamp
    Information Line)
www.fns.usda.gov/fsp

In the fiscal year 2000, the Food Stamp Program helped put food on the table for some 7.3 million households and 17.2 million individuals each day. The Food Stamp Program is a nutrition assistance program that provides low-income households with coupons they can use like cash at most grocery stores. The goal of this program is to ensure that families have access to a healthy diet. Food stamps can be used to buy many different food items, including baby food and cereal, bread, cheese and dairy products, and other food items for your baby and the whole family. The Food Stamp Program is administered by the U.S. Department of Agriculture at the federal level, through its Food and Nutrition Service. You can go to a local food stamp office to fill out an application or call the office and ask for an application to be sent to you. For more information about the Food Stamp Program and eligibility requirements, contact the U.S. Department of Agriculture at 800-221-5689. Go online for further details. The eligibility requirements to receive food stamps are posted at www.foodusa.org.

✿ GlaxoSmithKline

In the United States, call 800-546-0420

GlaxoSmithKline has two programs available to help provide medicines to those who don't have insurance: the SmithKline Beecham Foundation's Access to Care Program (available for those who do not have private prescription drug insurance) and the Glaxo Wellcome Program. Call for details on eligibility criteria and other information on these programs.

✿ SCHIP (The State Children's Health Insurance Program)

In the United States, call 410-786-3000 (sorry, not a toll-free number)

www.policyalmanac.org/health/chip.shtml

The purpose of the SCHIP program is to provide free or low-cost health insurance to uninsured, low-income children. All uninsured children who are ineligible for Medicaid are eligible for SCHIP. Go to www.hcfa.gov/medicaid/obs5.htm for a listing of state SCHIP toll-free numbers. For more information, go online or call.

✿ WIC (Women, Infants, and Children)

In the United States, call 703-305-2746 (sorry, not a toll-free number)

www.fns.usda.gov/wic

WIC is a government assistance program that offers outstanding assistance to eligible low-income families. This program serves 45 percent of all infants born in the United States. In fact, one in four new mothers participates in WIC. This program is available to low-income families and those who are nutritionally at risk. WIC will provide, free of charge, nutritious foods (such as infant formula, milk, bread, cheese, and cereal) during your baby's first years to needy families. WIC also provides free information on nutrition, breast-feeding, and education, as well as screening and referrals to other health, welfare, and social services. The program targets pregnant women (through pregnancy and up to six weeks after birth or after pregnancy ends), breast-feeding women (up to infant's first birthday), non-breast-feeding postpartum women, infants (up to the first birthday), and children up to their fifth birthday. WIC operates through two thousand local agencies in ten thousand clinic sites, in fifty state health departments, in thirty-two Indian Tribal Organizations, and in American Samoa, the District of Columbia, Puerto Rico, Guam, and the Virgin Islands. Services are provided at hospitals, community centers, public housing sites, and schools across the United States. The toll-free numbers and addresses for each state are listed on WIC's website. Click on "Contacts" to locate the contact information for your state, as well as to view the state's income eligibility guidelines. You can also call the number listed on page 133 to be directed to a WIC program in your state.

Free Financial Assistance, Tax Breaks, and Other Benefits in Canada

The government of Canada offers tax benefits and financial assistance to families to help with the cost of raising children, as well as provides educational counseling and support services for those in need. Check out the following listings for more information on these various programs, services, and entitlements and their eligibility requirements.

❀ **Canada Child Tax Benefit**
   In Canada, call 800-387-1193
   www.ccra.gc.ca/benefits

The Canada Child Tax Benefit (CCTB) is a nontaxable payment to help families with the cost of raising children. It is paid monthly to eligible families with children under age eighteen. The CCTB also includes the National Child Benefit Supplement (NCBS), which is a monthly benefit for low-income families with children.

For more information about these benefits, call for a free copy of the pamphlet *Your Canada Child Tax Benefit*, or download a copy at the website. You can also download a copy of this pamphlet at www .communication.gc.ca/children-enfants/02_e.htm.

❀ Canada Prenatal Nutrition Program
Health Canada
Finance Building
Tunney's Pasture
Ottawa, ON K1A 1B5
In Canada, call 613-952-0240 (sorry, not a toll-free number)
www.hc-sc.gc.ca/hppb/regions/ab-nwt/program/e_cpnp.html

The Canada Prenatal Nutrition Program helps community organizations provide services to at-risk pregnant women, including help with nutrition and breast-feeding, infant development, substance abuse problems, stress, family violence, and more. A variety of services are offered to improve birth outcomes for at-risk women, including nutritional counseling, food supplements, education, referrals, counseling on lifestyle issues, and more. You can find more information about this program at the website or by contacting the Canada Prenatal Nutrition Program. For a complete listing of CPNP Projects across Canada, visit the website and click on "Canada Prenatal Nutrition Program Projects Directory Online."

❀ Canada Site
In Canada, call 800-O-CANADA
www.canada.gc.ca

For current information about Government of Canada services, call or visit the website.

❧ Disability Tax Credit

In Canada, call 800-959-8281

www.ccra.gc.ca/disability

The Disability Tax Credit is a nonrefundable tax credit for people who have a "severe and prolonged mental or physical impairment." It is available to persons who support a child with a disability. For more information about the Disability Tax Credit, as well as eligibility requirements, call or visit the website.

❧ Easter Seal Society Financial Assistance Program

In Ontario, call 866-630-3336

www.easterseals.org/services/default.asp?load=direct

The Easter Seal Society offers financial assistance programs to families, children, and young adults with physical disabilities in Ontario. The society will assist with the cost of medical equipment purchases and rentals, as well as eligible services. Families must apply for registration to receive financial assistance from the Easter Seal Society. See the website or call for more details.

❧ *Employment Insurance: New Maternity, Parental and Sickness Benefits*

In Canada, call 800-O-CANADA

www.hrdc-drhc.gc.ca/ae-ei/pubs/special_e.shtml

Parents with a child born or placed in their care for adoption on or after December 31, 2000, may be eligible for increased parental benefits, including Employment Insurance, Maternity, and Parental Benefits for up to a year. The Government of Canada has also reduced the number of accumulated hours of insured employment necessary to qualify for these benefits from 700 hours to 600 hours.

The free pamphlet *Employment Insurance: New Maternity, Parental and Sickness Benefits* will answer your questions regarding maternity leave and parental benefits in Canada. Some of the topics covered include how to apply for benefits, who is eligible, the qualifying period, what information is needed to apply, and how long you can receive maternity benefits. Call to order a free copy of this publication, or log on to the website for more information.

❦ Federal Child Support Guidelines

www.canada.justice.gc.ca (click on "Programs and Services," then
   "Child Support")

The Federal Child Support Guidelines set out the basic amount that parents providing child support should pay based on income, the number of children involved, and the province or territory where the parents live. For more information about these guidelines, visit the website.

❦ Nobody's Perfect

In Canada, call 613-237-7667 (sorry, not a toll-free number)
www.hc-sc.gc.ca (click on "Just for You," then "Parents," then
   "Nobody's Perfect")

Parents of children from birth to age 5, who are young, single, or living in social, cultural, or geographic isolation or on a low income, as well as parents for whom parenting programs are not generally accessible, can receive support and education through the Nobody's Perfect Program. This program is offered as a series of six to eight weekly group sessions. For more information about this program, call your local public health department or community health center, or call the Canadian Association of Family Resource Programs at the above-listed number for further details. You can also check out the website for more details on this program.

❦ Ontario Child Care Supplement for Working Families

In Ontario, call
English: 800-263-7965 (Ministry of Finance)
French: 800-668-5821 (Ministry of Finance)

Qualifying families in Ontario are entitled to a monthly child care supplement from the government, according to their net family income.

These child care supplements are tax-free and do not have to be reported on your tax return. For more information on how you can receive this additional child care benefit from the government, call the Ministry of Finance's Information Centre.

✿ *Services for Children: Guide to Government of Canada Services for Children and Their Families*
In Canada, call 800-O-CANADA
www.communication.gc.ca/children-enfants/serv_e.htm

This free guide lists the many services that the Government of Canada offers to parents and caregivers and explains how to get more information on these services. It is an excellent resource, providing information on such topics as child health, safety, and nutrition; tax measures and benefits to help with the costs of raising children; services if your child or family has special needs; and educational resources. To order this free guide, fill out the online form or call.

✿ Tax Information Phone Services (T.I.P.S.)
In Canada, call 800-267-6999

This is a toll-free number that Canadians can call to help them determine whether or not they are eligible for the Canada Child Tax Benefit.

✿ Additional Tax Measures and Benefits
In Canada, call 800-959-2221

The following are other tax measures offered by the Government of Canada to help Canadian families with children:

• **Child care expenses.** You may be eligible to claim child care expenses on your tax return if you or your spouse or common-law partner paid for someone to care for your child so you could earn income from employment or self-employment, go to school, or do research during the year.

- **Equivalent-to-spouse amount.** You may be able to claim an equivalent-to-spouse amount on your tax return if you are single, divorced, separated, or widowed and support a child.

Call to find out more about these and other tax measures offered by the Government of Canada to help families with children. To receive forms to apply for any of these benefits, call. You can also go to www.ccra-adrc.gc.ca/formspubs/menu-e.html to obtain the required forms to apply for these benefits.

Parental Support

When my first daughter, Kayla, was born, I can't tell you all the times I was up in the middle of the night, simply checking to make sure she was breathing and lying safely on her back at all times. I worried about every little cough, sneeze, and sniffle. I kept wondering, "Is this normal?" "Is there something I should be doing?"

At times, I often felt that my concerns were silly, that I was just being an overprotective mom. But the truth was, there were many times that I really could have used someone to talk to about my concerns.

After calling some of the parenting support groups and organizations that follow, I was relieved to find out that my concerns weren't silly at all, and that, in fact, many new moms were experiencing the same concerns I had.

As a new parent, you are bound to be unsure of yourself and of what is best for your baby at times. Maybe you are having problems breast-feeding and can't get him to latch on properly, or maybe your baby is crying uncontrollably and you are wondering if she might have colic and what you can do to help, or maybe your baby has a fever and you are unsure of the medication to administer.

It's completely natural for a new parent to worry about these things. I can't name a single parent who hasn't. That's one of the reasons that I felt it necessary to compile a list of parenting support groups and organizations, most with toll-free numbers, for you to call, to give you someone to talk to when you have a parenting question or concern. These calls are free of charge, and many of these support groups and organizations are available 24/7.

For parents who don't know where to turn when a problem arises, the numbers listed in this chapter will put you in touch with trained professionals, including social workers and nurses, and parenting support group workers who can help you find the answers you are looking for. These professionals will address such concerns as breast-feeding, colic, SIDS, alcohol and drug abuse, AIDS, Down syndrome, premature births, adoption, family planning, and nutrition. Many of these groups and organizations also offer free programs and services, as well as free informational literature.

So in the middle of the night, even if you just need someone to talk to, remember that you are not alone. If you have a concern, no matter how small, give one of these groups a call. That's what they're there for. The staff at these groups or organizations are more than willing to help. And remember, there is no such thing as a stupid question. Call your doctor or get the help and support you need through these services.

As each situation is unique, the information provided by these support groups and organizations and their staff should not be used as a substitute for the medical care and personal attention of your physician or for any emergency situations.

❧ AAMR

In the United States or Canada, call 800-424-3688
www.aamr.org

AAMR promotes universal human rights for people with intellectual disabilities and provides help and support to families. Call for information and free educational literature.

❧ Americans with Disabilities Act

In the United States, call 800-514-0301

The U.S. Department of Justice provides information and free publications about the Americans with Disabilities Act (ADA) through the toll-free ADA Information Line. Specialists will provide general information about ADA, answer specific technical questions, or provide information about filing a complaint.

✿ America's Pregnancy Helpline
In the United States or Canada, call 888-4-OPTIONS
www.thehelpline.org

Call to receive free and confidential information about your pregnancy as well as sexual health–related issues. The toll-free number will link you to support groups and child care assistance programs. You can also visit the website to send an E-mail with your pregnancy-related questions to a pregnancy counselor, complete an online pregnancy test, and more.

✿ Association for Children for Enforcement of Support
In the United States, call 800-537-7072
www.childsupport-aces.org/home.html

Association for Children for Enforcement of Support (ACES), a non-profit child support organization consisting of concerned parents whose children are entitled to support, is dedicated to improving child support enforcement. ACES provides the free self-help handbook *How to Collect Child Support*, which includes information regarding collecting child support, visitation problems, child support laws, government agencies, and enforcement methods for collecting child support payments. There is a small membership fee (based on your income) to join ACES. However, ACES will waive dues for special circumstances. Go online or call for further details.

✿ Canada Pregnancy Hotline
In Canada, call: 800-665-0570

Call the pregnancy hotline to find answers to your pregnancy questions, including breast-feeding, abortion, and other areas of concern. When you call this number, they will help to connect and refer you to the closest crisis pregnancy center in your area.

❦ Child Find of America, Inc.

In the United States or Canada, call 800-426-5678
www.childfindofamerica.org

Child Find of America is a not-for-profit charity whose mission is to locate missing children and prevent child abduction. In the unfortunate event that your child might go missing, contact Child Find for assistance.

❦ Children and Adults with Attention-Deficit/Hyperactivity Disorder

In the United States or Canada, call 800-233-4050
www.chadd.org

Children and Adults with Attention-Deficit/Hyperactivity Disorder offers education, advocacy, and support for children and adults with AD/HD. The website provides information and resources about AD/HD.

❦ Council for Exceptional Children

In the United States, call 800-328-0272
www.cec.sped.org

The Council for Exceptional Children is available for persons concerned with the education of exceptional children. The organization provides educational, informational, and support services for handicapped and gifted children.

❦ The Danny Foundation

In the United States, call 800-83-DANNY
www.dannyfoundation.org

The primary focus of the Danny Foundation is to help prevent unintentional injuries by educating the public about crib dangers, as well as to set standards for safe nursery products. To be sure that your crib is safe for your baby and meets the current safety standards, check out the Crib Safety Checklist at the website. Call to receive a checklist and recall information by mail. This offer is available to residents of the United States only.

❦ Easter Seals
In the United States, call 800-221-6827
www.easter-seals.org

Easter Seals offers help and support to children and adults with disabilities. Services include helping children with disabilities succeed in school, helping people learn job skills and enter the workplace, rehabilitation services, as well as various other assistance programs. The children's services include infant monitoring programs to recognize developmental delays and help parents measure an infant's skills; affordable, high-quality child care; and help for infants born into substance-abusing families and infants born to teenage mothers. For more details, visit the website or call.

❦ Endometriosis Association
In the United States, call 800-992-3636
In Canada, call 800-426-2END
www.endometriosisassn.org

The Endometriosis Association is an organization that offers help, support, and pertinent medical information to women with endometriosis. Call to find out about the free endometriosis-screening program, as well as to receive general information about endometriosis.

❦ Family Service Canada
In Canada, call 800-668-7808
www.familyservicecanada.org

The mission of Family Service Canada is "to promote families as the primary source of nurture and development of individuals, to promote quality services which strengthen families and communities, and to advocate policies and legislation which advance family well-being in Canada." The organization provides a wide range of services, programs, and resources for families and individuals in Canada.

❦ The Jesse Cause Foundation

> In the United States or Canada, call 805-984-7933 (sorry, not a toll-free number)
>
> www.groupbstrep.com

Group B Strep is the number one infectious killer of newborn infants in the United States. Some babies have died within days or weeks of birth; others have suffered terrifying brain surgeries, loss of sight and hearing, as well as reduced mental or physical aptitude, according to the Jesse Cause Foundation. The Centers for Disease Control and Prevention state that close to 90 percent of these tragedies can be prevented by giving pregnant women a noninvasive test and treating them with antibiotics during labor. As many people haven't heard of Group B Strep, and as some doctors are still not routinely screening or educating women about the risk of it, the Jesse Cause Foundation places emphasis on universally testing every pregnant woman and raising public awareness about this infectious killer. Call or visit the website for more information.

❦ Johnson & Johnson Pediatric Institute, L.L.C.

> In the United States, call 877-JNJ-LINK
>
> In Canada, call 314-216-3560 (sorry, not a toll-free number)
>
> www.jjpi.com

One phone call to the Johnson & Johnson Pediatric Institute will give you the most up-to-date information on today's parenting topics from the expertise of thousands of specialists from around the world. The organization offers a variety of easy-to-understand booklets and videos on child development and parenting.

❦ **La Leche League Canada**

   In Canada, call 800-665-4324

   www.lalecheleaguecanada.ca

   La Leche League is a priceless resource for moms who breast-feed. The organization offers up-to-date information on breast-feeding, including how to know when your baby is getting enough milk, how to know when it is time for a feeding, what types of food a breast-feeding mother should eat, how to store expressed breast milk, and more. Call for references and referrals in your area or visit the website for current breast-feeding information.

❦ **La Leche League International (U.S.)**

   In the United States, call 800-LALECHE

   www.lalecheleague.org

   La Leche League is the only organization with the sole purpose of helping moms who breast-feed. The organization has some three thousand local groups in the United States, which meet regularly to share breast-feeding information and mothering experience. It is a priceless resource for all moms who breast-feed. You can get up-to-date information on breast-feeding, including the correct positioning of the baby at the breast, how to know when your baby is getting enough milk, how to know when it is time for a feeding, what types of food a breast-feeding mother should eat, how to store expressed breast milk, and more. Call to receive telephone counseling, as well as to receive references and referrals in your area. Visit the website for current breast-feeding information.

❦ **Make-A-Wish Foundation**

   In the United States, call 800-722-WISH

   www.makeawish.org

   The goal of the Make-A-Wish Foundation is to grant the wishes of children with life-threatening illnesses. If you know a child with a life-threatening illness, please call the Make-A-Wish Foundation.

❦ March of Dimes

In the United States or Canada, call 888-MODIMES

The March of Dimes Pregnancy and Newborn Health Education Center is a great place to call when you're expecting. Pregnancy information experts will answer your questions on pregnancy, birth defects, and more. You can also call to receive a special packet of materials for parents and families who have experienced the loss of a child between conception and the first month of life.

❦ Motherisk

www.motherisk.org

Motherisk is available to provide information and guidance to pregnant or lactating moms regarding the safety or risk of drugs, chemicals, diseases, infections, and other exposures during pregnancy.

- **Alcohol and Substance Use in Pregnancy helpline:** In the United States, call 416-813-8738 (sorry, not a toll-free number). In Canada, call 877-FAS-INFO. This help line will provide pregnant and breast-feeding women and their families with information on alcohol and substance use in pregnancy, including the possible effects of alcohol and other substances on their baby.

- **General Exposures in Pregnancy and Breastfeeding:** In the United States or Canada, call 416-813-6780 (sorry, not a toll-free number). It is probably still safe for you to breast-feed your baby even if you are taking medication. If you are unsure about the effect of a medication on breast-feeding or pregnancy, call Motherisk for information.

- **HIV Healthline and Network:** In the United States or Canada, call 888-246-5840. Call to receive confidential counseling about the risk of HIV and about HIV treatment in pregnancy, as well as for access to information and care for women on issues involved in HIV infections during pregnancy and breast-feeding.

- **Nausea and Vomiting in Pregnancy helpline:** In the United States or Canada, call 800-436-8477. According to Motherisk, "Nausea and vomiting in pregnancy (NVP), also referred to as 'morning sickness,' is very common. It afflicts up to 80 percent of pregnant women, to a greater or lesser extent." Call for support and information about morning sickness, including its effects, ways to help alleviate morning sickness, and answers about care and treatment.

National Adoption Center
In the United States, call 800-862-3678
www.adopt.org

The National Adoption Center works with social workers and other adoption professionals to bring children and families together throughout the United States. Adoption professionals list available children and interested families and make matches between them. If you have a completed home study and are approved to adopt, you can register on the National Adoption Exchange. The center also offers information and referral services, and it provides resource materials and adoption information packages on a variety of topics. Call for further information.

National Down Syndrome Society Hotline
In the United States or Canada, call 800-221-4602
www.ndss.org

The National Down Syndrome Society has a toll-free help line that parents can call to get general information about Down syndrome, as well as referrals to local parent support groups. New parents can call and request a free new parent packet.

National Information Center for Children and Youth with Disabilities
In the United States, call 800-695-0285
www.nichcy.org

NICHCY is a national information and referral center. It provides information on disabilities and disability-related issues for families, with a special focus on children and youth from birth to 22 years of age. You can call to speak to an information specialist, as well as to receive publications and fact sheets on specific disabilities, resource sheets, parent guides, and more.

❦ The Nurturing Network

In the United States or Canada, call 800-TNN-4MOM
www.nurturingnetwork.org

The Nurturing Network is an international charitable organization with more than thirty-two thousand volunteer members who have provided for the immediate, practical needs of nearly fifteen thousand women facing the crisis of an unplanned pregnancy. The Nurturing Network offers individually tailored, life-saving resources to women whose own support networks have let them down, with special emphasis on assisting college and working women. This comprehensive support includes professional counseling, medical services, residential assistance, and educational, employment, and financial resources. The network invites clients and volunteers in the United States and Canada who either need help or can offer help to call for further information.

❦ Our Missing Children

In the United States or Canada, call 877-318-3576
www.ourmissingchildren.ca

Our Missing Children, a program created by the Government of Canada, provides assistance to parents when their children go missing. Resources include a photo-aging service, investigative assistance, and international networking.

❦ Parent Help Line

In Canada, call 888-603-9100
www.parentsinfo.sympatico.ca

The Parent Help Line is Canada's first national, bilingual toll-free phone counseling and referral service for parents and caregivers. It gives parents a place to turn for any parenting concerns, 24/7. It was developed by leading experts to give guidance, information, and support to parents of children aged 0 to 19. When you call, you will receive confidential advice from professionally trained counselors. The Parent Help Line also provides you with a library of recorded messages on hundreds of parenting issues.

❧ Parents Without Partners
In the United States or Canada, call 800-637-7974
www.parentswithoutpartners.org

Parents Without Partners is a resource for single parents and their children. The organization has chapters in both Canada and the United States and is the "largest international, nonprofit membership organization devoted to the welfare and interests of single parents and their children." Chapters run educational activity, family activity, and adult social/recreational activity programs, as well as featuring discussions, study groups, and professional speakers. Call or log on to the website to find a Parents Without Partners chapter in your area.

❧ Poison Control
In the United States, call 800-222-1222

Keep this number by your phone or posted on your fridge. When you dial this toll-free hotline, you'll automatically be connected to the closest poison control center. You can call this number 24/7 to talk to a poison expert or if you have a poison emergency. This toll-free number is available to residents of the United States only.

❧ Poison Information Centres
The following are hotlines to reach the various Poison Information Centres in Canada:

Alberta: 800-332-1414
British Columbia: 800-567-8911

Manitoba: 204-787-2591
New Brunswick: 506-857-5555
Newfoundland: 709-722-1110
Northwest Territories: 867-669-4100
Nova Scotia: 800-565-8161
Ontario: 800-268-9017
Quebec: 800-463-5060
Saskatchewan: 800-363-7474
Yukon: 867-667-8726

❀ Pregnancy Centers Online
www.pregnancycenters.org

At Pregnancy Centers Online you can talk to a pregnancy counselor by E-mail, receive post-abortion counseling, as well as view a listing of toll-free pregnancy help hotlines and pregnancy care centers in the United States and Canada.

❀ RSV Hotline
In the United States or Canada, call 877-906-7085

A premature infant can be at an increased risk for serious RSV (respiratory syncytial virus) disease. For more information about RSV and what can be done to prevent it in premature infants, call the hotline.

❀ Salvation Army
In the United States or Canada, call 800-SAL-ARMY
www.salvationarmy.org

If you are in need, this number will connect you to your local Salvation Army for information on current programs and services that are offered, in the areas of volunteer services, day care referral, drug and alcohol counseling, emergency and disaster, prayer and counseling, missing persons, and more. You can also call this number to make a charitable donation or arrange for a thrift store pickup.

❦ SIDS Alliance

In the United States or Canada, call 800-221-7437

The SIDS Alliance provides information on sudden infant death syndrome and explains the correct sleeping positions for infants, as well as other important facts that you need to know to reduce the risk of SIDS and suffocation. Call for further information on SIDS, as well as to request free SIDS literature.

❦ Spina Bifida Association of America

In the United States or Canada, call 800-621-3141
www.sbaa.org

Spina bifida results from the failure of the spine to close properly during the first month of pregnancy. According to the Spina Bifida Association of America, "Spina bifida is the most frequently occurring permanently disabling birth defect. It affects approximately one out of every 1,000 newborns in the United States." Having the goal of promoting the prevention of spina bifida, the Spina Bifida Association of America provides a toll-free number that offers information and referral service, as well as publications relating to spina bifida and information regarding the importance of folic acid in women trying to conceive.

❦ Telehealth Ontario

In Ontario, call 866-797-0000

At Telehealth Ontario, a registered nurse is available 24/7 to answer all of your health-related questions.

❦ Transport Canada

In Canada, call 800-333-0371

A forward-facing child seat is completely anchored only when the top strap is securely tethered to the vehicle. If you can't find your vehicle's tether anchorage, call Transport Canada for assistance, as well as to receive information on other motor vehicle and road safety issues.

❦ Women Work! The National Network for Women's Employment

In the United States, call 800-235-2732
www.womenwork.org/about.html

Women Work! offers more than one thousand education, training, and employment programs to women across America. This program helps women find jobs to support their families and helps them to achieve economic self-sufficiency. Check out the website or call for further information or to request a resource pack containing referral information. This program is available to residents of the United States only.

Saving for Your Baby's Future

According to the Canadian Scholarship Trust Plan, it is estimated that in the year 2019, a four-year degree will cost $151,000 Canadian or $75,000 U.S.—ouch! Although it may seem like a long time away at this point, it is definitely a good idea to start saving as soon as possible for your child's education, spreading the payments out over several years.

There are many different types of savings programs available. Speak to a financial adviser to find the one that suits you and your family the best. Keep in mind that you don't need to invest a large amount of money—some of the programs available require only a minimal monthly investment.

BabyMint
www.babymint.com

Parents who join the free BabyMint Program can save for their child's future education every time they make purchases at hundreds of leading retailers. The BabyMint Program is a free college savings program that allows parents to save up to $50,000 for their child's college tuition. With each purchase you make at a participating retailer, a cash-back contribution is earned and then automatically deposited into an education investment account set up for your child. Retailers' contributions can go as high as 20 percent of your total purchase and are automatically deposited into your account. Grandparents and other relatives of the family can also join and direct their BabyMint cash-back earnings to your child's savings account. Visit the BabyMint website to receive more details and to complete a membership application. This program is available to residents of the United States only.

❦ Canada Education Savings Grant Program

In Canada, call 888-276-3624

www.hrdc-drhc.gc.ca (click on "Children and Youth," then "Canada Education Savings Grant")

More than 1.5 million Canadians have opened a Registered Education Savings Plan (RESP). With the Canada Education Savings Grant Program, you can start saving for your child's education now and receive an extra 20 percent contribution from the Government of Canada. Check online or call for details.

❦ Gerber Life Grow-Up Plan

In the United States or Canada, call 800-311-2055

www.gerberlife.com

The Gerber Life Grow-Up Plan is designed to provide life insurance protection to children between 14 days and 12 years of age. Call to receive a free Gerber Grow-Up Plan insurance information packet and application. This offer is available to residents of the United States and Canada.

❦ Upromise

www.upromise.com

Upromise is a free college savings program. Thousands of companies participate in this program and will contribute a portion of what you spend with them to your Upromise account to help you save for college. Some of the participating companies include Toys "R" Us, Babies "R" Us, Kids "R" Us, Staples, Borders, Waldenbooks, Exxon, and Mobil, to name a few. You will also receive a college savings contribution when you buy particular grocery items at your local participating grocery store, when you dine at various restaurants, including McDonald's and more than seven thousand other restaurants, as well as when you shop online. Grandparents and friends can also contribute to your college savings account.

The website offers a Search box to help you find participating stores in your area. Go online for further details on how you can open up a free Upromise account. This savings program is available to residents of the United States only.

Mom's Free Stuff

Mom's had a hard day—to put it mildly! Baby decided to wear his cereal bowl as a hat at breakfast. When the mailman arrived at the front door with the mail at lunch, baby said his first word, "da-da." And while at the grocery store in the evening, baby pulled one of your Tampax feminine products out of your purse at the checkout counter, waving it through the air like a baton!

A day in the life of a new mom isn't always easy. It seems like children are at their most exuberant when their parents are the most exhausted. There are bound to be those pull-out-your-hair type of days when nothing seems to go right.

In the midst of all the chaos and endless diaper changes, sometimes it seems that we forget about ourselves. It is important for new moms to try to take care of themselves as much as possible and to take time out to recharge and reenergize.

Because you deserve a break now and then, I've added some free items for you to pamper yourself with—some luxury bath products to help you unwind, free makeup, hair and perfume samples, recipes, cool savings, plus a ton of other terrific freebies I think you'll really enjoy.

Beauty Products to Pamper Mom

The following companies offer free beauty samples from time to time. Visit their websites or call their toll-free numbers. If offers are not available the first time around, check back frequently, as many of these companies will relist an offer at a future date or add an even newer promotional item for you to try out.

❧ **Almay**

www.almay.com/register.asp

Register online to get special notice about Almay's new products, contests, free samples, coupons, and more. This offer is available to residents of the United States and Canada.

❧ **Apple a Day**

www.appleaday.com (click on "Free Trial Samples")

Sign up to receive a free trial sample of the "New You" Skin Rejuvenation System, created to give you healthy, smooth, younger-looking skin. This offer is available to residents of the United States and Canada.

❧ **Arbonne and Mertzlufft & Associates**

www.mertzlufft.com (click on "Free Samples")

Fill out an online form to receive free samples of skin care products. This offer is available to residents of the United States and Canada.

❧ **Club Med**

www.clubmedbeauty.com

Log on to the Club Med website to receive a free sample of My Ocean fragrance or other current promotional offers. This offer is available to residents of the United States only.

✿ Cover Girl
www.covergirl.com

Log on to Cover Girl's website to enter contests, receive free makeup samples off and on throughout the year, and more. This offer is available to residents of the United States and Canada.

✿ DHC Skincare
In the United States, call 800-DHC-CARE
www.dhccare.com/retail (click on "Sample Request")

DHC Skincare offers a free body care sample kit, the Olive Essentials Sample Kit, featuring sample sizes of Deep Cleansing Oil, Mild Soap, Mild Lotion, and Olive Virgin Oil. A shipping fee of $2 is applied to all sample-kit-only orders when you order online. You will also get a $5 gift certificate good toward your next order. However, you can avoid the $2 sample kit shipping fee by calling the toll-free number to order. (Sample requests taken by phone will not include the $5 gift certificate.) This offer is available to residents of the United States only.

✿ Dove
In the United States or Canada, call 888-393-2444
www.dove.com

Call Dove Deodorant's Free Sample Request Line to receive a free trial-size sample of Dove's new deodorant or another promotional item. This offer is available to residents of the United States and Canada. Residents of the United States can also receive a free Dove sample online at the Dove website.

✿ Dream Perfumes
www.dreamperfumes.com

Dream Perfumes is offering several free perfume samples for you to try.

- Bitch is "a new wild and seductive fragrance" from Gosh International. Order a free sample at www.houseofgosh.com/bitch.htm.
- K-A-O-S is a new fragrance from Gosh International "that will turn your world upside down." Order a free sample at www.houseof gosh.com/k-a-o-s.htm.
- Ottomane is a "warm and sensual fragrance" from Ulric de Varens. Order a free sample at www.houseofgosh.com/ottomane.htm.
- rue Pergolese is a fragrance from Ulric de Varens, named after a quaint side street in Paris. Order a free sample at www.houseofgosh.com/ruepergolese.htm.
- Varensia is a "fruity floral with a gently entrancing fragrance" from Ulric de Varens. Order a free sample at www.houseofgosh.com/varensia.htm.

These offers are available to residents of the United States only.

❦ Enchantress Hosiery

www.enchantresshosiery.com/free/default.asp

To introduce you to its fine line of hosiery, Enchantress will send you a free pair of Enchantress pantyhose. Check out the website for details. This offer is available to residents of Canada only.

❦ Free-Beauty-Samples.Com

www.free-beauty-samples.com

Free-Beauty-Samples.Com will send you free makeup and a daily newsletter just for joining. This offer is available to residents of the United States only.

❦ Free Cosmetics

www.1freebieaday.com/free_cosmetics.html

At this website you can receive cosmetics, beauty products, and fragrances absolutely free. Go online for details. This offer is good for residents of the United States only.

✽ Head & Shoulders

www.headandshoulders.com/usa/free_samples

Complete an online questionnaire to receive a free sample of a new Head & Shoulders shampoo. This offer is available to residents of the United States only.

✽ Highway International

www.highwayinternational.com (click on "Free Sample!")

Chewitt is a disposable toothbrush that is chewed! While you are chewing, all parts of the teeth are cleaned simultaneously. Fill out the online form for a free sample. This offer is available to residents of the United States and Canada.

✽ Kiwi International Products

www.kiwiproducts.co.nz

Join Kiwi International Products' mailing list to be kept up-to-date with new products and free samples. This offer is available to residents of the United States and Canada.

✽ Masada

www.masada-spa.com/feedback.html

All of Masada's fine spa products contain 100 percent natural, unprocessed mineral salts from the Dead Sea. For more information about this company, and to receive a free sample packet of one of their products, fill out the form at the Masada website. This offer is available to residents of the United States and Canada.

❦ Maybelline
www.maybelline.com/smp/index.html

Fill out Maybelline's online form to receive special offers, free samples, and the inside scoop on products and promotions. This offer is available to residents of the United States and Canada.

❦ MyBeautyCenter
www.mybeautycenter.com (click on "Special Offers")

At MyBeautyCenter, you can sign up to receive various free makeup samples. This offer is available to residents of the United States and Canada.

❦ Olay
www.total-effects.com/sample/sample.shtml

This website offers free samples of Olay skin-care products or other current promotional items. This offer is available to residents of the United States only.

❦ Physique
www.physique.com/keep (click on "Join Club Physique")

When you join Club Physique, you will get a free Physique sample sent to you, plus samples of some upcoming products. This offer is available to residents of the United States and Canada.

❦ Pureology Serious Color Care
www.pureology.com/bsfreesamples.html

Pureology offers hair care products that preserve and protect color-treated hair. To receive free samples of Pureology products, fill out the form on the website. This offer is available to residents of the United States and Canada.

✿ Q-tips
In the United States, call 888-668-4391

Call to receive a free travel pack and makeup tips or other free promotional offers. This offer is available to residents of the United States only.

✿ Razzamatazz
c/o DNA Enterpres
P.O. Box 185711
Hamden, CT 06518
www.razzamatazz.net/question.php

Print out and mail in Razzamatazz's online questionnaire, along with $1.99 to cover the shipping and handling costs, to receive a free hair consultation and trial gift package. Visit their website where you will find the pertinent details. This offer is available to residents of the United States only.

✿ Rembrandt Oral Care Products
In the United States, call 800-548-3663
www.rembrandt.com

Rembrandt offers free product samples and discount coupons for money off Rembrandt Oral Care Products periodically throughout the year. Call to request a free sample or coupon. This offer is available to residents of the United States only.

✿ Renova
www.wrinklereport.com/gift/index.html

Register online to receive a free Renova Skin Therapy Information Kit and $10 in savings. This offer is available to residents of the United States only.

❧ **Skin Care Magic**

www.freemakeupsamples.4t.com

This website offers a free Skin Care Magic sample. Check out the website for further details on how you can receive your free sample. This offer is available to residents of the United States and Canada.

❧ **Sonya Dakar**

www.sonyadakar.com/skin-chart.htm

Sonya Dakar offers online visitors a complimentary skin consultation and a free gift by mail. Visit the website for more details. This offer is available to residents of the United States only.

❧ **Uncle Harry's Natural Products**

www.uncleharrys.com (click on "Sample Request")

Uncle Harry's Natural Tooth Powder is made of 100 percent natural ingredients. Fill out the online form to receive a free sample. This offer is available to residents of the United States and Canada.

❧ **Unilever**

In Canada, call 800-279-9317

Call to receive a free Caress Silkening Body Lotion sample or another free promotional item from Unilever. This offer is available to residents of Canada only.

Free Recipes and Recipe Books

Why go out and buy expensive cookbooks when you can get tons of fabulous recipes and recipe books for free! The following companies offer lots of great recipe ideas that your whole family will enjoy.

✿ Allrecipes
www.allrecipes.com

The Allrecipes website presents an assortment of great recipes, meal ideas, and cooking advice. Categories in the recipe collection include appetizers, brunch, quick and easy meals, desserts, holiday cooking, and more.

✿ Canned Food Alliance
www.mealtime.org

The Canned Food Alliance recipe database contains hundreds of healthy recipes, complete with preparation time, cooking time, and nutritional information.

✿ Dare Foods
www.15minutestofame.com/recipes.htm

This website features some great recipes from Dare Foods. These recipes take fifteen minutes or less to prepare.

✿ Domino Sugar
www.dominosugar.com

The Domino Sugar website is filled with great recipes and great fun for you and your kids. There are ideas for delicious meals for your family, including dips and spreads, appetizers, salads, desserts, and more.

✿ Eden Foods
www.edenfoods.com

Eden Foods, a natural and organic food company, lists more than four hundred recipes on its website. You can search for recipes by type of meal, by culture of origin, or by recipe contents.

❧ FamilyTime

www.familytime.net

At this website you will find great ideas for recipes, meals, entertaining, and family fun. Of the more than four thousand recipes are some from Campbell's, McCormick, Nestlé, and Swanson, as well as recipes listed by region, including Asian, Italian, Mediterranean, and others.

❧ Fresh Del Monte Produce Inc.

www.freshdelmonte.com (click on "Free Stuff")

At this website you can download the *Del Monte Hawaii Gold Pineapple Cookbook* for free.

❧ Hidden Valley

In the United States, call 800-723-2343

Call to receive a free recipe collection from Hidden Valley. This offer is available to residents of the United States only.

❧ Land O'Lakes

In the United States or Canada, call 800-782-9602
www.landolakes.com

Hundreds of free recipes, meal ideas, and baking tips are available at the Land O'Lakes website. You can also receive a free Land O'Lakes recipe book by calling. This offer is available to residents of the United States and Canada.

❧ M&M's

In the United States, call 800-627-7852
In Canada, call 888-709-6277
www.m-ms.com/us/baking

Call for a free M&M's recipe book. You can also check out the M&M's website for yummy M&M's recipes your kids will love, including cakes, brownies and bars, ice cream, delicious cookies, and other sweet treats. This offer is available to residents of the United States and Canada.

❀ Reynolds Kitchens

www.reynoldskitchen.com (click on "Order Brochures")

Reynolds Kitchens offers free brochures with great tips, hints, and ideas. Fill out the online form to receive a selection of brochures. Tons of delicious, free recipes are also available for you to view at this website, with topics including "Cooking for Company," "Delicious Desserts," "On the Grill," and more. This offer is available to residents of the United States and Canada.

❀ Sunsweet

In the United States, call 800-417-2253

Call to receive free recipes from Sunsweet. This offer is available to residents of the United States only.

❀ Swanson

www.swansonbroth.com/cookbook_offer.asp

The free Swanson Broth cookbook *Simply Delicious* contains twelve new recipes and "Tricks of the Trade." You can order this free cookbook online. This offer is available to residents of the United States only.

For the Craftsy Mom

Crafts and hobbies can be a great way for parents to unwind and relieve stress, and they allow you to explore your creative side and try something new.

The following websites offer free craft projects and craft sheets that you can print out from your computer. If you're great at sewing, there are even some online patterns you can use to make your own baby clothing and accessories.

❀ 1 Stop Free Shop

www.1stopfreeshop.com/craftpatterns.htm

There are hundreds of free craft patterns to choose from at this website, such as birdhouse patterns, candle patterns, folk art patterns, floral patterns, paints and painting patterns, and more. Photos, materials needed, and complete instructions are also included.

❀ AllCrafts

www.allcrafts.net

This terrific site is a crafter's dream come true. At AllCrafts you will find hundreds of free craft projects, in many different categories, including holiday crafts, kids' crafts, nature crafts, candle- and soap-making crafts, rubber-stamping, scrapbooking, and more. You will also find tons of free craft patterns that you can print out.

❀ Ben Franklin

www.benfranklinstores.com (click on "Projects")

An assortment of free craft project sheets, which you can print out, is available at the Ben Franklin website. The supplies that you will need are listed, and the instructions to complete these craft projects are given.

❀ Cloth Doll Connection

www.clothdollconnection.com/FreePatterns.html

At the Cloth Doll Connection, you can print out free cloth doll patterns. There are several different patterns to choose from. Instructions and supplies needed to complete these projects are also featured.

✼ Craftown
www.craftown.com

The craftsy mom will find everything she needs at this terrific website, which features country, Victorian, and holiday crafts, instructions for candle and jewelry making, as well as free craft patterns, including crochet, knitting, quilting, kids' craft patterns, and more. The website also offers free online tutorials where you can learn a new crafts skill at the learning center.

✼ Free Craftz Patternz
www.freecraftz.com

This excellent crafter's website offers tons of free craft patterns, including online tole painting patterns, free folk art patterns, and woodworking projects, as well as adorable country angel and Raggedy Annie patterns that you can simply print out. Links to other crafting websites are provided as well.

✼ Martingale & Company
www2.martingale-pub.com/freepatterns/default.htm

This crafts website offers free patterns and instructions for quilters, knitters, and crafters that you can print out.

✼ Sue's CrochetandKnitting.com
www.crochetandknitting.com/patterns.htm

Visit this website to print out patterns to make crocheted baby socks and slippers for your infant.

Just for Fun

Head over to the Virtual Chocolate website to check out the mouthwatering selection of delicious, heavenly chocolate. Then surf over to the Mail a Meal website to check out the selection of free gourmet meal postcards you can send to your favorite friends in cyberspace. The fun doesn't really begin until you dream the day away at the Virtual Presents website, where you can imagine owning a brand new Porsche or taking an exotic vacation. You can even send these free virtual presents as postcards to someone special!

You'll find some really fun and tasty websites in this section. So grab a cup of tea or coffee, sit down, and check out these websites—just for fun! (Keep in mind, while you're surfing through the Virtual Chocolate site, that I love chocolate, too—hint, hint!)

❧ 2CoolBaby
www.2coolbaby.com/12ROSES.htm

This website offers printable coupons aimed at busy parents who have very few intimate moments together. There are twelve romantic coupons to choose from, including "Full Body Massage," "Breakfast in Bed (served wearing only a smile)," "Candlelit Bubble Bath," and more. Take time out to enjoy these coupons with your spouse!

❧ AmericanGreetings.com
www.americangreetings.com

AmericanGreetings.com offers a terrific selection of free online greetings in such areas as friendship, recipes, and love and dating. Also available is a huge selection of really cool music greetings, courtesy of BeatGreets, with more than three hundred artists to choose from! Many of the greetings at this website are animated. You can include a personal message on your greeting and send it via E-mail to someone special. And if you'd rather send a card by snail mail, click on "Free Coupon" for a coupon you can print out and redeem at participating retailers.

❧ Freebies for Women
www.freebiesforwomen.com/notepads.shtml

The Freebies for Women website features several free notepads for you to print out and use. Some are for grocery shopping lists and errands, others are just for doodling. You can print out as many of these funny and original notepads as you like.

❦ Mail a Meal
www.mailameal.com

Mail a Meal is a fun website for sending free food and gourmet meal postcards to friends and loved ones on the Net. There are several categories to choose from, including caviar, shrimp and lobster appetizers, gourmet desserts, tropical drinks, candlelight and romantic dinners—even a complete Thanksgiving roast turkey dinner! There's enough delicious gourmet food on this website to make anyone's mouth water. Mmmm!

❦ Mom's Break Village
www.momsbreak.com (click on "Iron-On Transfers")

The Mom's Break website offers a large assortment of free iron-on transfers that you can print out on transfer paper. Some of the cute sayings for your transfers are as follows: "Grandmas Give the Best Hugs," "Grandpas Give the Best Hugs," "Mommy . . . Where Do Babies Come From?," and "But Daddy Said It Would Be OK!" At this website you will also find free baby shower games, baby announcements, and baby shower, pregnancy, and kids' birthday printables, including invitations, iron-on transfers, and more.

❦ A Mom's Joy
www.amomsjoy.com

Give the gift of love. Print out your free "love coupons" at this website. Choose from such fun and romantic coupons as "Coupon for a Kiss," "Coupon for One Good Laugh," "Free Babysitting," "Queen for a Day," "Free from Housework Coupon" (now we're talking!), "Coupon for an Evening of Romance" (works for me!), and more. These coupons are a great way to say "I love you."

❧ Original Country Clipart by Lisa
www.countryclipart.com/recipecards.htm

This website offers some cute country recipe cards, shopping lists, gift tags, and to-do lists that you can print out for free.

❧ Virtual Chocolate
www.virtualchocolate.com

Chocolate lovers will definitely love this website. You can send luscious and heavenly virtual chocolate treats, chocolate electronic postcards, and more to a favorite friend in cyberspace. So much mouth-watering chocolate to choose from!

❧ Virtual Presents
www.virtualpresents.com

Virtual Presents is a fun website for sending free virtual presents as postcards to friends and loved ones on the Net. You can choose from extravagant, luxury items such as a brand-new Porsche, dream vacation photos, a romantic bouquet of flowers for your sweetheart, even a brief-case full of money. A great place to dream the day away.

Miscellaneous Freebies

The following are a few miscellaneous freebies, including catalogs, parenting freebies, and other various samples for the home.

❧ Carnation Instant Breakfast
www.carnationinstantbreakfast.com/free_sample.asp

Sign up online to receive a free sample of the newest flavor of Carnation Instant Breakfast. This offer is available to residents of the United States only.

❦ Claritin

In the United States, call 888-833-0003
www.claritin.com/rebatesoffers/index.html

Claritin Syrup relieves seasonal allergy symptoms in children age 2 and older. Call for a free $5 rebate certificate and product information. The Claritin website also offers other rebates off and on throughout the year. Check back at a later time if an offer is not currently available. This offer is available to residents of the United States only.

❦ EverythingForParents.com

www.everythingforparents.com/bookmark.htm

Request a free Everything for Parents bookmark at this parenting website. These bookmarks present information about other parenting websites (ePregnancy, GeoParent, and Myria) on one side. A guide to Internet message board abbreviations appears on the other side. This offer is available to residents of the United States and Canada.

❦ Excedrin

In the United States, call 800-EXCEDRIN
www.excedrin.com

Call or visit the Excedrin website to be added to the Excedrin mailing list to receive a free Excedrin Migraine brochure and sample. This offer is available to residents of the United States only.

❦ Frederick's of Hollywood

In the United States or Canada, call 800-323-9525
www.fredericks.com/shopdepartment.asp (click on "Catalog")

To receive a free catalog featuring lingerie, bras, panties, clothing, shoes, legware, and other accessories, fill out the online request form or call. This offer is available to residents of the United States and Canada.

❦ Healthmall.com

www.healthmall.com (click on "Free Vitamins")

When you fill out an online survey, you can enter a monthly contest to win a free one-year supply of vitamins and herbs. This offer is available to residents of the United States only.

❦ Kiddie Kobbler

www.kiddiekobbler.com/coupons.htm

Visit the Kiddie Kobbler website to print out $5 discount coupons for Kiddie Kobbler children's shoes.

❦ Martha Stewart Living Omnimedia, Inc.

www.marthastewart.com

To receive a free Martha Stewart catalog featuring products for cooking, gardening, entertaining, crafting, traveling, kids, babies, and more, request one from the website (click on "Catalog Requests"). This offer is available to residents of the United States and Canada.

In the United States and Canada, call 800-999-6518 to request a free trial issue of the *Martha Stewart Living* magazine to look at, with no risk or obligation to buy. Call for further details. This offer is available to residents of the United States and Canada.

❦ No Brainer Blinds and Shades

Free Safety Offer
4660 Beechnut
Suite 218

Houston, TX 77096
www.nobrainerblinds.com/info/child.html

Write to No Brainer Blinds and Shades to receive free cleats or breakaway safety tassels. These cleats and tassels are designed to help prevent
strangulation from window treatment cords. Include a self-addressed,
stamped envelope with your request. Be sure to affix proper U.S. postage
with a minimum of 43¢ postage for residents of the United States, and
two Canadian postage stamps if you reside in Canada. The company will
send you either two breakaway tassels or two cleats at no cost other than
the stamps. Write the word "tassel" or "cleat" on the return envelope, *not
on your envelope to them*. This offer is available to residents of the United
States and Canada.

For more information on making today's window treatments
safer for young children, visit the website.

❀ Pepcid Complete
www.pepcidcomplete.ca/en/trialoffer/index.asp

Complete a brief survey at the website to receive a free trial-size
sample of Pepcid Complete Chewable Tablet for heartburn relief,
together with a coupon for your next purchase. This offer is available to
residents of Canada only.

❀ Slim-Fast Foods Company
In the United States, call 877-375-4632
www.slim-fast.com

Sign up online to join the free Slim-Fast Club and receive access
to Weight Charting Tools, notification of special promotions and
coupon offers, a free newsletter subscription, and more. This offer is
available to residents of the United States and Canada. Residents of
the United States can also call to request a free *Guide to Healthy Living* brochure.

Something to Remember Me By
www.somethingtoremembermeby.org

Something to Remember Me By is a legacy project designed to encourage closer relationships between parents, grandparents, and children. Free online activity theme kits are available at different times of the year. These activity kits are filled with intergenerational activities, crafts, a listing of books and websites that grandparents and grandchildren can share, and much more. Some of the different activity theme kits include Grandparents Day, The Holidays, Valentine's Day, Mother's Day, and more. To get a free online copy of the latest activity kit that you can view or print out, visit the website. This website also offers free Grandparent Awards that you can print out for your child to give to her grandparents, as well as free Best Mom Award certificates, printable note cards, and more.

StartSampling
www.startsampling.com

Sign up online to request a free sample of Downy Enhancer or other promotional items. This offer is available to residents of the United States only.

Susan G. Komen Breast Cancer Foundation
In the United States or Canada, call 800-462-9273
www.komen.org

The Susan G. Komen Breast Cancer Foundation offers a free breast self-exam instruction card that is waterproof and can be hung in your shower. This handy reminder card illustrates and describes the techniques of breast self-examination. Call the Breast Care Helpline at the above-listed toll-free number to request a free card. You can also call the Breast Care Helpline for information about breast exams and breast cancer. This offer is available to residents of the United States and Canada.

❧ Tide Fabric Care Network
www.tide.com/specialoffers

This website offers free samples and contests from time to time throughout the year. If a free offer is not currently available, check back again at a later time.

❧ T-Stick Disposable Thermometers
www.t-stick.com/freesample.htm

The T-Stick is a single-use cardboard thermometer that is used to quickly check if meat, fish, or poultry is thoroughly cooked. To receive a free sample, send a self-addressed, stamped envelope to:

Free T-Stick Sample
Trans World Services, Inc.
72 Stone Place
Melrose, MA 02176

❧ Ultrafem
In the United States or Canada, call 877-367-9636
www.softcup.com (click on "Samples")

Ultrafem's Instead SoftCup is a feminine protection product. It is not a tampon or pad but rather a soft little cup that you wear internally. Call or visit the website to order a free Introductory Club Kit, which includes three SoftCups, an instructional video, and valuable coupons. (This offer is free, but a shipping and handling price of $3.50 (U.S.) is applied for the kit to be sent to you.) This offer is available to residents of the United States and Canada.

❧ Victoria's Secret
In the United States or Canada, call 800-HER-GIFT
www.victoriassecret.com (click on "Request a Catalogue")

To request a free catalog from Victoria's Secret, call or visit the website. This offer is available to residents of the United States and Canada.

❦ Walt Disney World

In the United States or Canada, call 800-793-2640

Planning a trip to the Magic Kingdom? Call to receive a free "100 Years of Magic" video to help you make the most of your Walt Disney World vacation. This offer is available to residents of the United States and Canada.

Ways to Stretch Your Dollar

I remember, back in my "BD" (before diapers) days, a girlfriend telling me how things had changed drastically from the birth of her first baby to the birth of her now third baby.

With her first baby she told me that she went on a clean streak, sterilizing everything from bottles to nipples, rattles to teething rings. When her first baby dropped his pacifier on the floor, she would immediately sterilize it in boiling water for several minutes before handing it back to him. But with the birth of her second baby, she eased up quite a bit. This time when her baby dropped his pacifier on the floor, she would pick it up, run hot water over it, and then hand it back to him. By the time her third baby came along, she simply picked the pacifier up off the floor, put it into her mouth, and then handed it back to the reaching arms of her baby. I remember thinking, "Bad Mommy! Bad Mommy! I'll never be so careless with my baby."

True to my words, when my first daughter, Kayla, was born, I, too, sterilized anything and everything that would even come in contact with her. I always bought the most expensive laundry soap, packaged especially for babies, in the rare case that my daughter would develop an insidious rash from the regular family laundry soap. I prewashed all of her brand-new baby clothes immediately after taking them out of the packages. I always gave my daughter a bath every day, sometimes twice a day if she was really dirty, and I was always sure to change her outfits the minute they were messy.

But my quest to be a perfect mom didn't stop there. I must have read more than ten parenting books before my daughter was even born to be sure I was extra prepared in absolutely every situation. *What to Expect When You're Expecting* was my bible. I poured over and clipped out articles from parenting magazines and—don't laugh at me when I tell you this—even neatly arranged the articles in file folders according to various categories (e.g., baby food, sleep, nursing, etc.).

In my quest to be Supermom, I bought every gizmo and gadget on the market (many of them are still collecting dust in my closet). I spent a fortune on the latest baby toys, only to find that my baby enjoyed playing more with my car keys, the remote, and my cordless phone, not to mention the boxes and wrapping that all those expensive baby toys came in. As far as clothing went, I always tried to make sure that my daughter was dressed from head to toe in a perfectly matched, spotless ensemble.

Now, with the birth of my twins, I, too, have eased up in many ways. I give my babies a bath every two or three days and a quick sponge bath on the days they don't get a bath if they are really dirty. (That alone saves me tons of time and energy!) On wash days I throw my babies' outfits in the laundry with the rest of the family's dirty clothes, using my regular family laundry detergent, and they still come out smelling sweet and clean. I graciously accept hand-me-downs from friends and relatives, as well as whatever help and support they so kindly have to offer. As far as clothing goes now, sometimes I'm lucky if my babies are even wearing any, especially in the summer when it's really hot outside. But babies love to be naked, I reason, and they sure are adorable running around the yard naked as jaybirds, happy as larks!

In fact, I try to do whatever I can to make my life easier and am always looking for the simplest and best way to do things.

As a mother of three, I definitely feel that I'm more confident and don't find myself worrying so much about all the little things. Does it really matter if my child isn't weaned from her bottle by the time she reaches her first birthday? Do you really think my babies care if they're wearing hand-me-downs or the latest designer fashions?

There are, of course, still many things that I draw the line on, especially when it comes to safety issues. Our house is like Fort Knox. I wouldn't have it any other way. Every cupboard is locked, medicines are tucked away safely, baby gates guard the top and bottom of the staircases, safety covers are plugged into all the outlets. These things are too important to be overlooked.

I also set limits on the things that I feel are important to my children, like insisting that they wash their hands after going to the bathroom, say "please" and "thank you" as much as possible, clean up their toys at the end of the day, and—please—stay out of the toilet bowl!

My children just love books, crafts, and music. I always try to take time out to read to them or do a craft project with them every day. These are the things that I personally won't scrimp on, as they are the things that provide my children the most enjoyment and, to me, are essential.

I think that, as each parent is different, you have to decide for yourself what matters the most to you and what doesn't, what your priorities are and what you can let slip occasionally, what would make your life a little easier, and what would give you more time with your children, more time for yourself—and more sleep!

As far as obsessing about keeping the house clean, forget it. There are going to be many times when it will be next to impossible to keep your house clean—and besides, do you really have to finish the dishes when your daughter has just created her first finger painting masterpiece and wants you to help her proudly display it on the fridge?

Financially, you have to learn how to question your purchases ("How much could I save if I switched from one brand to another?") as well as to resist your urges and impulses ("This baby shampoo costs twice as much as the other one, but it smells so much better."). And most important, you have to learn to do what makes you feel comfortable, not what you feel is expected of you from others.

When Kayla was born, I made some very expensive (ouch!) mistakes. But like they say, experience is the best teacher, and I have learned a few little tricks and tips along the way that I would like to share with you to help you, too, save money and hopefully give you more quality time to spend with your precious new little one.

Here are some mommy-tested-and-approved ideas from a been-there-done-that mom who, after making some expensive mistakes the first time around, went on to save hundreds, if not thousands, of dollars when the twins were born.

Diapers

Babies go through a ton of diapers. Some days it seems like they poop twice their body weight! In the first three years of your baby's life, diapers will probably be one of your biggest expenses, as your baby will need more than six thousand diaper changes during this period.

Stock Up

As you can never have enough diapers, it's a good idea to start buying diapers early. Here's a great way to stock up on diapers in advance. When you get into about the fourth or fifth month of your pregnancy, start buying one package of diapers every week or every other week when you do your regular grocery shopping. Skip the newborn-sized diapers—you will probably only need one or two packages of them anyway—and buy the larger-sized diaper packs.

When we found out that we were expecting twins, we started buying diapers right away, one pack a week from my third month of pregnancy on, and when the twins came, we definitely knew that we had made a smart choice. Not one of those diapers went to waste!

Buy in Bulk

Another way to save on diapers is to buy direct from the factory at warehouse prices. Give the factory or warehouse a call in advance and ask if the public can make bulk purchases directly from the warehouse at a discounted rate. (This goes for other baby items as well.)

Check your local flyers to see when diapers go on sale in your area and stock up.

Warehouse stores like Cosco also offer a great deal on diapers when you buy them by the case. Shopping this way can really save you a bundle!

Cloth Diapers

Cloth diapers seem to be becoming popular again. New accessories, such as cotton diaper wraps, diaper covers, and even felted wool diaper covers, are now available for your added convenience as well. When you buy cloth diapers, not only will you be saving money, but you won't be adding to the landfill problem.

Diaper Pails

Being the mother of twins, I always had a difficult time trying to keep the babies' nursery smelling sweet with all the diapers the twins would go through. Here's a simple and inexpensive trick that I learned from another mom on how to eliminate diaper pail odors. Save all of your plastic grocery bags and empty bread bags. Put the dirty diaper into one of these bags, tie the bag in a knot, and toss it into your diaper pail. This method works similar to a Diaper Genie by keeping the odors locked in, except that it's free!

Formula

Another big expense in your baby's first year of life, should you decide not to breast-feed, will be formula. There are a couple of simple ways that you can cut the costs of formula, ways that will really add up in the long run.

One way to save money on infant formula is by purchasing a store-brand formula instead of a name-brand formula. There are many store-brand formulas available, depending on where you do your shopping, and many of them are made by Wyeth Nutrition, including Parent's Choice Infant Formula, a great formula that you can purchase exclusively at Wal-Mart. These store-brand infant formulas can be up to 40 percent cheaper than the national name brands, saving you as much as $500 (U.S.) on the cost of formula in your baby's first year alone!

Many parents have the misconception that the cheaper formulas will not meet the nutritional needs of their baby, and that the more expensive brands have more to offer, but the truth is that the less-expensive formulas contain almost the same ingredients as the more costly formulas.

To ensure that you are getting the best quality formula for your baby, no matter what price you are paying, the Infant Formula Act requires all baby formula manufacturers to follow specific procedures and guidelines when they make their formula. The ingredients found in infant formula are strictly regulated. The only difference is the price consumers pay.

You can also save money on the cost of infant formula by choosing powder formula over the more expensive concentrated liquid formula. The preparation of powder formula may require a little extra effort, but it will really save you money in the long run.

Baby Food

When your baby first begins to eat solids, she will only need a small amount of baby food per feeding. In the first few weeks it will seem like a lot of that leftover baby food goes to waste as it has to be thrown out after a couple days of being left in the fridge.

To preserve the leftover baby food, pour the food into the individual compartments of an ice-cube tray. Cover with plastic wrap and freeze. Once it's frozen, pop it out, put the cubes in a resealable bag, and place the bag back into the freezer. Take one or two cubes out each night, depending on the amount that your baby will need for the next day, and put them in the fridge to thaw overnight.

These individual cubes are the perfect size portions for your baby when she first starts on solids. With this method, you'll no longer have to spend the extra money buying the more expensive smaller-sized baby food jars and you can buy only the larger sizes, without worrying that anything will go to waste.

Another great way to save money on baby food is to make your own. Homemade baby food can help you provide low-cost, nutritious food for your little one.

Making your own baby food is really simple. You can puree the baby food in a blender or food processor and pour it into the individual compartments of an ice-cube tray in the same manner as just discussed. Another great thing about making your own baby food is that you know exactly what is going into it—no added salt, sugar, or starch and no unnecessary spices.

So get to work on your purees for some nutritious meals that your baby will love!

(For some great recipes for making your own nutritious, homemade baby food, check out the online recipes from Chapter 2, "Baby Freebies on the Net.")

Breast-Feed and Save

Breast-feed, and give your baby the best for nothing!

There are so many wonderful benefits to breast-feeding, both to you and your baby—financial benefits as well. Moms who breast-feed their babies can save more than $1,000 (U.S.) a year in formula alone! Breast milk is free—it doesn't cost a penny. Should you choose to breast-feed, there are other things that you will save money on as well, including baby clothing (because formula stains can ruin an outfit and they are difficult to remove) as well as the cost of baby bottles and nipples.

Breast-feeding is definitely the best choice for your baby for many reasons.

Benefits to Baby

1. No baby formula measures up to mother's milk. Breast milk provides perfect infant nutrition. It also provides added protection against illnesses and diseases.
2. Breast milk helps pass meconium. Colostrum, or early milk, is designed to help move this sticky tarlike substance through an infant's body.
3. Breast milk is fresh. It is also more digestible than formula, as human milk contains an enzyme that aids in digestion.
4. Studies have shown that formula feeding increases a baby girl's risk of developing breast cancer in later life. Women who were breast-fed as children had a 25 percent lower risk of developing breast cancer than women who were bottle-fed as infants.
5. Studies have shown that formula feeding is associated with a lower IQ. Those who were breast-fed as infants had both better intelligence and greater academic achievement than children who were infant-formula fed.
6. While breast-feeding, Baby benefits from close body contact with mother.

And if all of that's not enough reason for you to breast-feed, think of the benefits to yourself as well.

Benefits to Mom

1. Your body returns to its prepregnancy size faster. Lactation burns nearly five hundred calories a day, which results in quicker weight loss.
2. There is less postpartum bleeding in women who breast-feed their infants.
3. Breast-feeding for 34 months or more in your lifetime lowers the risk of certain cancers, reduces the risk of premenopausal breast cancer by 35 percent.
4. Breast milk is free!

5. Breast milk is readily accessible and is always warmed and ready to go. No formula to make, no bottles to sterilize, and no mess to clean!

If you are getting frustrated and are having problems breast-feeding your infant, don't give up! Contact La Leche League (listed in Chapter 8, "Parenting Support Groups") for current breast-feeding information and tips.

Maternity Wear

When I was expecting my first daughter, I remember complaining to a friend that I had to buy expensive maternity clothes that I was only going to wear for a few months and possibly a second time if we decided to have more children. The next thing you know, my friend disappeared into her basement and reappeared with a huge box filled with maternity clothes. "Where did you get all of these clothes?" I asked. She told me that each of her friends at work who had recently given birth had passed on their maternity clothes for her to wear when she was expecting. She never had to buy a single maternity wear item, except for bras and underwear. "And now they're all yours," she said with a grin, dropping this huge box in front of me.

I was really glad to accept this unexpected gift from my friend, especially at a time when the endless list of things that I needed to buy for my baby was growing and growing. I wore a lot of the maternity clothing from that box when I was expecting. After my baby was born, I put all the clothes back into an even bigger box, added a few of my own purchases, and passed them all back to my friend, who then passed this now quite huge box to another one of her expecting friends.

Don't be shy to approach friends, coworkers, and relatives who have recently given birth and ask them if you can borrow their maternity clothes—chances are they won't mind a bit and will be glad that their maternity clothing can get more wear.

Then after you have given birth to your baby, put your maternity clothing in a box, and pass it on to another expecting mom. I'm sure she will really appreciate it!

Baby Clothes

When I found out that I was expecting, one of the first things I did was head out to the nearest Baby Gap and buy up almost everything in the store. I bought tons of onesies, sleepers, booties, hats, and bibs. Those adorable brand-new baby clothes are hard to resist—and so-ooo cute!

Next, I headed over to the nearest department store and stocked up on baby accessories, baby bedding, bottles, grooming kits—you name it. I spent an absolute fortune!

A few months later my best friend, Diane, threw me a baby shower, where I received tons of beautiful baby clothes and other precious baby gifts. Thanks to doting grandparents, my new baby's wardrobe was better than my own! I ended up with so much stuff for my baby, way more than I would ever possibly be able to use.

My advice to you is to wait until after your baby shower to start buying clothing for your baby to make sure you buy only the items you really need and to avoid duplication. Chances are you'll receive lots of beautiful baby outfits, sleepers, and other baby accessories at your baby shower, enough that you may not need to buy many new items yourself.

Another great idea is to register for your baby shower at Babies "R" Us, Toys "R" Us, Sears, or any other store that offers a free baby registry. When registering for a baby shower, you can list exactly what you need. Registering for your baby shower in advance also makes it easier for friends and relatives who are unsure of what to buy for the baby. (See "Drop-in Freebies" in Chapter 3, "Free Stuff from Stores," for a list of some companies that offer free baby registries.)

Get the word out that you will gratefully accept any and all hand-me-downs. Both of my sisters-in-law and my best friend gave me boxes and boxes of baby clothing. Most of the items were in excellent condition, some had never been worn, and the ones that had been worn were perfect to be used for outside play and for baby to wear around the house.

When I was pregnant with my twins, Shane and Katie, I was very lucky. I hardly bought any new outfits for my babies as I received tons of great hand-me-downs from friends and relatives. (It seems that when people find out you're expecting twins, clothing just seems to pop up from everywhere!) Most of the clothing that I did buy myself for the twins came from secondhand stores.

Secondhand Treasures

When my first daughter was born, the sky was the limit! I spent a fortune dressing her from head to toe in designer baby outfits. By the time my twins came, I realized I could no longer afford this luxury.

I have to thank my sister-in-law Kelly for getting me hooked on "second-time-around" stores. I highly recommend these stores for baby wear. You can find tons of designer baby clothing at these stores, for a fraction of the cost. Some of the clothing looks brand new and has hardly been worn. Many of these stores also carry slightly used baby furniture, as well as baby toys, accessories, swings, and more, usually in excellent condition.

So if you are lucky enough to find one of these stores in your neighborhood, you are well on your way to saving money.

Keep in mind that you can also sell baby's outgrown clothes to many second-time-around or consignment stores. Use this money to buy new clothes or other items for your baby.

Garage Sales

Another great way to get terrific deals on baby clothing is at garage sales. In our neighborhood on a Saturday morning, you can't make a simple trip to the convenience store without passing a garage sale. They're everywhere!

You wouldn't believe some of the great deals I've gotten at garage sales in my neighborhood. People were practically giving away their baby clothes. I bought huge boxes filled with baby clothes for only five bucks!

Buy Off-Season

A great time to buy baby clothing is off-season. Many stores put their winter clothes on sale during the late winter or early spring, and their summer clothing on sale during the late summer or early fall. You can get great deals buying off-season, sometimes even saving more than 50 percent off the original price.

Designer Clothes

I can't say I blame you for wanting to splurge on some adorable designer outfits for special occasions, but try to keep these purchases to a minimum, maybe one or two. Your baby will look absolutely adorable in that little velvet, lacy designer dress, but the spit-up will look the same as it did on that secondhand sleeper—and besides, you'll find that your baby will be much more comfortable in a 100 percent cotton sleeper than that itchy, scratchy, get-this-thing-off-of-me lacy dress!

Coupons and Discounts: Clip 'n' Save

One of the simplest and most effective ways to save money on baby products is to browse through your local newspaper for money-saving coupons on baby items. Ask your friends and family to clip out any baby product coupons that they find in magazines and newspapers and save them for you. The ones you don't need you can always swap with friends, relatives, or other mothers at work.

Online Coupons and Discounts: Click 'n' Save

Another great way to collect valuable discount coupons is through the Internet. The following is a list of websites that offer tons of free printable grocery coupons, retail coupons, coupons for baby products, and more. You can download and print out your coupons.

To make your online search for coupons and discounts quicker and easier, many of the sites listed offer a convenient search option, allowing you to hunt for a particular item by typing in a search word, such as "diapers," after which you'll be taken directly to a list of the companies that offer discount coupons on diapers. Many of these websites list their offers in several different categories (e.g., baby products, baby clothes, toys, groceries, and food coupons) to help direct you to exactly what it is you're looking for. Some websites even have special features where you can search for discounts and coupons in your area only, by state, province, or city.

Keep in mind that you should never have to pay a fee to get coupons online. Be wary of websites that request that you pay a monthly or a one-time fee to receive their coupons and discounts.

As mentioned earlier in the book, if you don't have access to a computer, either borrow one from a friend or try to get online at your local library, as many libraries now have Internet access available to the public at no charge. Happy hunting!

Bigcoupons.com
www.bigcoupons.com

Bigcoupons.com offers tons of free money-saving coupons—food coupons, retail coupons, and more—that you can print out. These offers are available to residents of the United States and Canada.

CoolSavings
www.coolsavings.com

CoolSavings offers grocery coupons, store coupons, free samples, gift certificates, rebates, and more. Sign up and save! This offer is available to residents of the United States only.

CouponSurfer.com
www.couponsurfer.com

At CouponSurfer.com, you can select coupons by clicking logos, browsing different categories, or doing a search. A wide assortment of online discount coupons is offered in several different categories, including baby and maternity coupons, books, clothing, food, grocery coupons, and more.

DailyeDeals.com

www.dailyedeals.com (click on "Online Coupons")

At this website you can search for money-saving coupons from many different websites that offer baby products, including the Disney Store, Gap, OshKosh B'Gosh, and more. You can find discounts on baby gifts, baby clothes, toys, children's books, and other baby stuff. Many of these websites have special clearance sales where you can receive a discount of more than 50 percent.

Dine4Less

www.dine4less.com

At this website residents of Canada and the United States can receive free discount coupons to save money at their favorite restaurants. Many of these restaurants offer free savings coupons, promotions, special offers, discounts, and diner clubs. For a complete listing of the offers available in your area, simply type in the name of your city, state, or province.

Factory Outlets

www.outletbound.com

At this website you can receive a free "Shop Like a Pro" VIP voucher redeemable at more than 160 participating outlet centers nationwide. Save hundreds of dollars the next time you go shopping! This offer is available to residents of the United States and Canada.

H.O.T! Coupons!

www.hotcoupons.com

When you register at this website, you will get an E-mail to let you know what coupons are available in your area. You can also search this website by category as well as by typing in your ZIP code or geographic location to find coupons in your area. This offer is available to residents of the United States only.

✿ Valpak
www.valpak.com

This website offers free printable coupons for the whole family! Just type in your ZIP code or postal code to see what is available in your area. This offer is available to residents of the United States and Canada.

Free Samples from Your Doctor

The next time you visit your doctor for a checkup, ask if any free samples are available to you and your family. Many doctors receive tons of free promotional samples and other items from time to time and would be glad to share them with you. Don't be afraid to ask.

If you suspect that you are pregnant and haven't yet purchased a home pregnancy test for confirmation, check with your doctor or local health clinic first, as most of them will provide you with a pregnancy test, free of charge.

Things You Should Never Buy Used

Don't scrimp on safety!

Crib

There are so many requirements that must be met by the companies that manufacture infant cribs, and for good reason. Cribs are associated with more children's deaths than any other juvenile product. According to the Danny Foundation, "Over 10,000 children are injured in unsafe cribs every year, seriously enough to require hospital treatment." A crib is something that you should never buy secondhand. An old crib may contain lead paint, which, if ingested, can be extremely dangerous. In addition, some of the slats on older cribs are too far apart and could entrap your baby's head. According to the U.S. Consumer Product Safety Commission, crib slats should be no more than 2⅜ inches apart. The mattress in your baby's crib should be firm and fit snugly and should not be too small for the crib, as your baby could accidentally slip in between the crib and the mattress. Make sure your crib meets the current national safety standards. (Visit the U.S. Consumer Product Safety Commission website, listed in Chapter 6, "Web Resources for Parents," for more information on product safety rules and regulations, as well as product recalls.)

Car Seat

The second thing that you should never buy used is an infant car seat. If a car seat has been in even a mild car crash, it may have been weakened and may not hold up in another crash. When you buy a used car seat, there is no way of knowing if it has been in a car crash. In addition, some of the older car seats may not meet today's safety standards. It's better to be safe than sorry.

Baby Swing

A baby swing is another thing that I do not suggest buying used or borrowing from a friend. According to the U.S. Consumer Product Safety Commission, "Each year about 1,200 children under age 2 suffer swing-related injuries."

There are several features that a swing should contain to keep it safe:

- A crotch restraint and a seat belt
- An adjustable seat that you can recline for a newborn and raise it as his neck gets stronger
- Speed control so you can choose a gentler, slower swing motion for a newborn and a faster swing motion for an older child
- Easy in/out access
- Braces between the legs of the swing for extra support

Some other things to keep in mind:

- Follow the safety instructions that accompany your swing.
- Do not attach toys with a long string to the swing.
- Do not put a pacifier on a cord around a baby's neck.
- Supervise and keep your baby in view.
- Stop using the swing once your baby can grab the swing's legs.

All-Time Best and Worst Baby Items

It's unbelievable, some of the extravagant baby items I've seen on the market over the last couple of years, popping up at upscale baby stores all over Canada and the United States. The "upscale baby," whose parents shop at these trendy stores, can be seen about town wearing luxurious leather suits and animal print dresses, suede-fringed jackets, designer jeans, and faux-fur jackets. These little tykes are really stylin'. Their wardrobes are better than my own.

One of the latest fashion trends to hit the market is perfume for babies. Hello? Are they serious? One of the things that I loved most about my babies was their sweet, natural scent. (I often found myself sneaking into their room while they were sleeping just to smell them. I couldn't help myself. They smelled so-ooo delicious!) As far as I'm concerned, no perfume can match that sweet, heavenly scent. But for the new baby, especially the firstborn, the sky's the limit.

When you are out shopping for your baby, the salespeople will make you think you need to buy everything. A new mom is an easy target, shopping at an emotional time and wanting to make sure that her baby has the best of everything.

The truth is, there are lots of things your baby can live without. You really don't need to have all the latest gizmos and gadgets on the market today.

The best thing you can do, before heading out to the department store, is make a list of the things that your baby *really* needs and stick to it. Stop buying things that *may* come in handy. They usually never do. When in doubt about what to buy, think about what baby items your mother used. I'm sure she didn't have near the amount of baby items that are on the market today, and she did just fine—didn't she?

My Top-Ten List of Totally Useless Baby Items

Think how much you could save by eliminating only a few, if not all, of the infant unnecessaries in the following list.

1. **Infant shoes.** Those little infant shoes certainly look cute in baby pictures, but an infant doesn't really need shoes until he is learning to walk. Skip 'em!

2. **Baby kimonos.** My husband calls them "The Hugh Hefner Designer Housecoat for Babies." Although they really do keep your baby all wrapped up and cozy-warm, a nice fluffy bath towel that is big enough to wrap your baby from head to toe is all you really need to keep your baby warm and dry after a bath.

3. **Baby powder.** Baby powder is a definite no-no. Besides the fact that it is unnecessary, it's also very dangerous and harmful to your baby's lungs if inhaled. Cross it off your shopping list. To keep baby dry, make sure you towel-dry your baby well after a bath. Be sure to get into all of the little cracks and crevices under the arms and legs. A layer of petroleum jelly is all you need to protect your baby's bottom from moisture. Frequent diaper changes will help to prevent diaper rash. If your baby does develop a serious diaper rash, zinc oxide is recommended by pediatricians.

4. **Crib bedding.** Pass up the $200 to $300 elaborate, showy crib bedding sets that include a comforter and a pillow. They look great in

a nursery, but according to the American Academy of Pediatrics, it is not recommended for baby to sleep with a comforter, pillow or other soft bedding. Babies should be put to sleep on their backs with a firm, flat mattress. This can help reduce SIDS (Sudden Infant Death Syndrome), as well as suffocation. All you really need to buy are a couple of fitted crib sheets.

5. **Changing table.** Many new parents think their baby's nursery isn't complete without a changing table. I had one and only used it once. To me, changing tables are the biggest waste of money. They are quite expensive and can take up a lot of space in the nursery, not to mention that they are dangerous as well. As strange as it may sound, the safest place to change a diaper is on the floor or on a bed with a washable plastic changing pad placed under your baby's bottom. No matter how wiggly your baby gets, it is impossible for her to fall off the floor. Most infants can wiggle themselves right off a changing table in a split second, which may result in serious injury or even death. Why take the chance? Keep in mind, too, that sometime after your baby's first birthday, she will probably be too big to change on the changing table and you'll end up changing her on the floor or bed anyway. But if you do have your heart set on getting a changing table, get a changing table/dresser combination that can be used by your child for many years to come.

6. **Receiving blankets.** I received well over ten receiving blankets at my baby shower. You really don't need that many. At home you can simply use a small towel to throw over your shoulder to protect your clothing from spit-up. A cloth diaper over your shoulder also does the same thing and is much less expensive. If you like, you can purchase one or two new receiving blankets for when you take the baby out, but this is one area where new parents tend to go a bit overboard.

7. **Brush and comb set.** They make nice keepsakes but aren't really necessary. The last time I looked, most babies don't have a lot of hair. But if your baby is born with massive amounts of beautiful hair, any clean comb or brush with soft bristles will do the trick.

8. **Baby carriers.** You don't need a baby carrier separate from your car seat. Spend your money on a good combination car seat/carrier. The best thing about these car seats is when your baby falls asleep in the car, you simply remove the baby carrier from the car seat and carry baby inside the house, without having to wake him up by taking him out of his car seat.

9. **Cradle or bassinet.** You really don't need a cradle or bassinet if your baby's crib will fit in your room. When our twins were born, they slept in their separate cribs in our room until they were big enough to be moved into their nursery. You only use the cradle for a very short period of time anyway, as most babies only fit in them for a few months. My advice to you is to spend your money on a good solid, adjustable crib.

10. **Bathtub seats.** Both useless and dangerous, infant bathtub seats are rings that are designed to keep your baby sitting upright in the bathtub. They can be quite dangerous as the suction cups on the seats can come unstuck, allowing the baby to easily tip over into the tub. There have been reported cases of babies drowning while using bathtub seats and rings. I had one but only used it once. It was uncomfortable and awkward for my baby, and besides, it was much more fun for me to take a bath together with my baby! But if you should decide to use one of these seats, *never* leave your baby alone in the bathtub, not even for a second.

Knock these useless baby items off your shopping list and save your money for the things you will really need to buy, like diapers—*lots of diapers*!

I'd Love to Hear From You

Send me an E-mail, or write to me with your list of totally useless baby items and I may post them on my website or even use them in my next book. (See the Introduction for my contact information.)

Things You Can't Do Without

The following is a list of some of the things you may want to have readily available when you arrive home with your new baby, as well as some of the items that will make your life easier in the first year of your baby's life.

1. **Diapers, diapers, diapers!** Let's face it—life without diapers would be . . . well . . . very messy!

2. **Onesies.** One-piece baby outfits, or onesies, are great because they won't slide up your baby's back. These combo T-shirts and bottoms won't pull up like regular T-shirts, plus they help to hold the baby's diaper in place. The best type of onesies to buy are the ones with snaps at the baby's crotch, making diaper changing much easier. Buy the adjustable ones with different snap positions that will allow the outfit to grow with your baby. You'll definitely need lots of these, but wait until after your baby shower to buy them, as you will probably get lots of them as gifts.

3. **Baby bibs.** One of the things that you'll want to stock up on when you're having a baby is baby bibs. You will need lots of baby bibs for when your baby spits up and starts on solids. My babies often kept their bibs on throughout most of the day. I found that it was much easier to simply put on a fresh new bib than to change their entire outfit every time they spit up. It also saved me money, as their outfits would stay newer and cleaner for a longer period of time. Fewer outfit changes = less laundry!

4. **Safety items.** Safety items for your home are essential, something you definitely don't want to scrimp on. Children have a wonderful sense of curiosity that, unfortunately, may get them into trouble. Be sure to take the time to go through your home carefully to find all the areas that might be unsafe for a little one. Get down on your hands and knees and inspect your home from top to bottom, using a baby's-eye view. Some of the items you should consider purchasing to help baby-proof your home are outlet covers to protect curi-

ous little fingers, cabinet latches, drawer locks and latches, baby gates, and toilet locks. (For a couple of simple ideas on making your own electric cord holders, baby choke testers, and more, see Chapter 13, "Why Buy It When You Can Make It?")

5. **Nursing bra.** If you are planning on nursing your baby, you're going to need a good nursing bra. In my opinion, any nursing bra that you can't unfasten with one hand in one second is useless. When your baby is fussy and crying because he's hungry, you don't want to be messing around with a bra that is difficult to unfasten. Spend a little extra money to buy a good nursing bra, and wait until your last month of pregnancy to be sure of the most accurate sizing. Playtex and Motherwear both have excellent, highly rated nursing bras that will meet all of your needs.

6. **Bouncy seat.** Infant bouncy seats are priceless! They provide a safe place to put your baby and are really convenient, as they can be situated in any room of the house. They also come in handy when your baby first starts on solids. As your baby probably won't be able to sit upright in the high chair at this point, you can feed your baby right in the bouncy seat. We used the vibrating type of bouncy seat, which always helped to put our babies to sleep. The attached musical toy bar was an added bonus, as the lights and music kept our babies entertained.

7. **Jolly Jumper or ExerSaucer.** Another safe place to put your baby while you are busy, perhaps in the kitchen preparing meals, is a Jolly Jumper or an ExerSaucer. Once your baby is big enough, a Jolly Jumper that you can hang in the doorway, or an ExerSaucer that you can place in the kitchen or any other room of your house, can be a great place to put your baby, providing lots of fun and entertainment, as well as exercise, for your little one.

8. **Waterproof changing pad.** You'll definitely get lots of use out of these! To protect your crib sheets from accidental leaks while your baby is sleeping, place a waterproof changing pad directly under your baby's bottom. You might also want to purchase an extra one

to carry in your diaper bag to always have a clean place to change your baby when you are out in public. You can use them on the floor or on the bed—actually, you can use them anywhere—to change your baby! Many of these changing pads also come with a separate removable cotton or flannel cover that you can put over the pad. It can easily be removed and simply thrown into the laundry when it gets dirty.

9. **Breast-feeding cream.** If you're going to breast-feed, I highly recommend using breast cream. I used it when I nursed all three of my babies. It really helped with cracks and sore nipples. Lansinoh makes a great breast cream that is made with pure lanolin. It is perfectly safe for baby as well.

10. **Rompers.** Rompers look so adorable on the little ones! Rompers with the feet are great to help keep your baby's feet warm at night and throughout the day—which comes in handy, since it's almost impossible to keep a pair of socks on a baby for any length of time.

I'd Love to Hear from You

Send me an E-mail or write me with your list of baby items that you can't do without, and I may post it on my website or even use it in my next book! (See the Introduction for my contact information.)

Why Buy It When You Can Make It?

There are tons of ways you can save money on baby products, arts and crafts, toys, baby clothing and accessories, and safety items. Be resourceful. Take a look around your home for items that can double as baby toys. Use ingredients you can find in your own kitchen cupboard to make terrific arts and crafts for your little one. Be creative and use your imagination to make all sorts of creative cost-saving baby items!

Baby Products

Here are some great money-saving ideas to make your own brand of baby products, including baby wipes, diaper rash cream, child safety items, diapers, and more. They are simple to make and great to use in a pinch when your supplies start running low.

Emergency "Diaper"

All out of diapers and baby needs to be changed, now? Use a cotton T-shirt. Any size will do, but the bigger the shirt, the better the absorbency.

Place the T-shirt on a flat surface. Fold in the sides to form a tapered end (cross over each side in the middle) at the T-shirt hem. Place baby's bottom on the center of the T-shirt, and wrap the sleeves around baby's tummy. Bring tapered end up, fold over overlapped sleeves, and tuck in. Pin securely.

Emergency Diaper Cover

Need a diaper cover in a hurry, and they're all in the wash? Use a plastic bag.

For a baby weighing less than 16 pounds, cut a "T" shape out of a grocery bag; use a garbage bag for a bigger baby. Cut the bottom part of your "T" about 10 inches (25 centimeters) wide on the bottom fold of the plastic bag. This will be the crotch part of your emergency diaper cover. Cut the top part of your "T" across the width of the plastic bag. This will be the waist ties. Make your "T" about 8 inches (20 centimeters) high for small, 10 inches (23 centimeters) high for medium, or 13 inches (33 centimeters) for large. Cut the sides of your "T" curved, for better coverage. Cut open the waist ties so you can tie it on over baby's diaper. Ties can be about 20 inches (51 centimeters) long for small, 23 inches (58 centimeters) for medium, or 27 inches (69 centimeters) for large. Trust me, it sounds more complicated than it is. . . .

When you open up the cover, you should have a giant "H" shape. Place a folded prefold diaper inside, place baby on top, and tie at each side of baby's waist.

If you really like this style of diaper cover, you can cut some more out of waterproof, ripstop nylon for no-sew, indestructible, washable tie-on diaper covers.

Diaper Rash Remedy

Thanks to Jennifer for this Frugal Baby Tip. I would like to share an idea for preventing diaper rash and chafing. I use aloe vera, either the fresh plant or the extract bought at the pharmacy or health food store. It saves money and is a great barrier cream. It also works great on teething rash around the mouth, as it is not harmful to swallow.

Baby Wipes (1)

Here's a great idea that all moms should know about—how to make your own homemade baby wipes.

Cut a large paper towel roll in half the round way. You will have two circles that are each about the size of a roll of toilet paper. (Use good quality, thick paper towels.) Next, mix together 2 cups warm water, 2 tablespoons baby oil, and 2 tablespoons baby bath or baby shampoo. Put one of the paper towel rolls into an empty container with a lid or an empty baby wipes container. (Use one of the half paper towel rolls per batch.) Pour the liquid mixture directly on top of the paper towel roll and cover. After the liquid has completely saturated the entire roll of paper towels, remove the cardboard tube. Pull your wipes from the middle of the roll. Keep sealed. Voilà!

Baby Wipes (2)

Thanks to J. Buffett for this Frugal Baby Tip. Use facial tissues for your baby's bottom, rather than the homemade baby wipes, to save money. I have a squirt bottle filled with 2 to 3 tablespoons baby wash, 2 to 3 tablespoons baby oil, and 2 cups water. I squirt his bottom, then wipe with the dry tissues.

Baby Laundry Bag

Thanks to Beth for this Frugal Baby Tip. Use an old pillowcase for a laundry bag in the baby's room. I attach it to the changing table by a diaper pin. It keeps all of baby's dirty things together, and when it's time to wash, everything can be dumped right into the washing machine, including the pillowcase!

Toilet Roll Protector

Save that toilet paper! To prevent your toddler from unrolling the entire roll of toilet paper and stuffing it into the toilet, make your own toilet roll protector by recycling a plastic 2-liter pop bottle. Cut the bottle top and bottom off to form a toilet roll cover about 4¾ inches (12 centimeters) wide. Cut a slot in this cover, to pull the toilet paper through, about ½ inch (1 centimeter) high and 3 inches (7½ centimeters) across. Remove your toilet roll and spindle from the wall mount, slide both inside your new toilet roll protector, and reattach to the wall mount. This should at least slow your toddler down!

Economical Baby Bassinet

Thanks to Candace for this Frugal Baby Tip. For families who cannot afford a bassinet, wicker laundry baskets make great substitutes.

With my oldest son, I used a wicker laundry basket as a bassinet, and I kept it beside my bed at all times. I could take it to the living room or anywhere else I needed as well. With my other two children, I used my plastic laundry basket and lined it with several layers of blankets to use as a place to keep them by my side during the day.

Stuffed Toy Net

Here's an idea to make your own "net," which will match your baby's nursery decor and hold all of baby's stuffed toys.

Just cut out a triangle of strong, stretchy fabric measuring about 40 inches by 40 inches by 60 inches (or 1 meter by 1 meter by 1½ meters). Tie each corner of this triangle tightly to a metal ring and suspend up in one corner of your baby's room with hooks screwed into the wall. Fill with those toys!

Nursery Bookends

Thanks to Renata for this Frugal Baby Tip. Make bookends out of stuffed animals. Undo the back of the stuffed animal. Take out some stuffing and fill with marbles. Resew by hand. To prevent sliding, glue some rubber matting on the bottom of the toy. This works great for matching the decor in your baby's room.

Hair Detangler

Does your child have tangles from baby-fine hair? Rather than buying those expensive bottles of spray-on detanglers, try making your own frugal alternative. Mix 1 part conditioner with 10 parts water. (You may need to experiment. Some conditioners work better for this than others.) Pour into an empty, cleaned-out spray bottle. Spray this frugal detangler solution on your child's hair, and comb those tangles out easily.

Nonslip Cup

Wrap one or two wide rubber bands onto your child's cup before you hand it to her. The rubber bands will give your child a better grip, and the cup won't slip out of her hands as easily.

Baby Choke Tester

Every home should have a choke tester to check if toys and other objects are safe for baby play. Commercial choke testers can be very difficult to find, very expensive, and too small to be effective.

Did you know that you already have a frugal baby choke tester right in your own home? (No, I don't mean the baby. . . .) An empty toilet paper tube!

Commercial choke testers are made to the government regulation size of $1\frac{3}{8}$ inches in diameter. However, the U.S. Consumer Product Safety Commission has reported many deaths of babies and children who have choked on objects slightly larger in diameter than this.

Your ordinary toilet paper tube is $1\frac{5}{8}$ inches in diameter. You can consider any toy or object in your home that fits inside this tube to be a choking hazard to your baby or child.

Cord Holders

Extra-long electrical wires, including extension cords and phone cords, may trip your little one—and are tempting for your baby to tug or chew on. Cord holders will hold those loose wires snugly against the wall.

Just cut two or more pieces of sticky-back Velcro 1 inch (5 centimeters) wide and about 2 inches (10 centimeters) long. Place the Velcro pieces with the sticky-back side along your baseboard, or wall, wherever the cord runs along, 1 to 2 feet (30 to 60 centimeters) apart. Stretch your cord out tight, and place the other side of the Velcro over the top of each piece attached to the wall, to hold the cord in place. Use as many pieces of Velcro as you need to hold the cord securely to your wall.

Childproof Bottle Tops

When your childproof bottles are empty, save the bottle tops. Wash them out and store in your kitchen drawer. When you buy something in a bottle that you wouldn't want your child to get into, but it doesn't come with its own childproof top, just check your childproof bottle-top stash for a bottle top that fits! Some pharmacies will also give you a childproof bottle top free, upon request.

Baby Clothing and Accessories

For those of you who are good at sewing, put your sewing skills to use and save money by sewing your own baby clothing, baby bibs, curtains and accessories for the nursery—even nursing and maternity wear. Fabric stores carry a great selection of patterns for adorable baby outfits and nursing wear. Choose a simple pattern and reuse it over and over again, choosing an assortment of different fabrics.

Following are a few simple ideas to make your own baby clothing and accessories.

Baby Mittens

Thanks to Arlene for this Frugal Baby Tip. Forget about those tiny mittens for winter babies. Use older brother's or sister's woolly socks—clean, of course! They pull up high enough that baby can't get them off easily, and snow can't get in either.

Instant "Bib"

All you'll need are two "suspender" clips and about 10 inches (25 centimeters) of fabric elastic to be able to make a bib for your baby, instantly, wherever you are. Just fold each end of the elastic around the loop of one of the suspender clips and stitch. Now you can use this handy gadget to clip a washcloth (or two, for heavy droolers!) or hand towel around baby's neck. You can also store it in your diaper bag for use on the go, using it with napkins at restaurants and other places.

Easy Baby Rompers

Make your baby a really cute-looking romper from an older child's T-shirt or tank top. Just make sure the hem of the shirt hangs a few inches lower than the baby's diaper crotch.

Stitch 2 to 3 inches (5 to 7½ centimeters) of Velcro loop (or two to three snap "heads") on the inside of the hem, center front, and 2 to 3 inches of Velcro hook (or two to three snap "holes") on the outside of the hem, center back. If you find the neck opening a bit too big, just overlap the fabric at the back of the neck, and add a dot of Velcro or one snap to hold it closed. Then you just slip your new baby romper on your baby and fasten at the crotch. How adorable!

Free Nursing Pads

Take an old cotton T-shirt and cut it up into 6-inch (15¼-centimeter) circles. Place three to six circles on top of each other, and sew two rows of stitching near the outer edge, about ⅛ inch apart, to prevent the edges from unraveling. These make very comfortable nursing pads that won't slide around as much inside your bra.

Less Slippery Socks

Thanks to Lisa for this Frugal Baby Tip. As your baby is just starting to learn how to walk and it is cold in the evenings (the reason for not being barefoot), instead of buying socks with grips on the soles already, buy the socks in the bulk bag and use puffy paint on the soles. If applied properly, it doesn't peel off (if you're worried about this, you can also get the nontoxic kind). You can write anything you want on the soles of the socks, or draw pictures, and baby will have a better grip on the floor.

Arts and Crafts

When your baby is well past the stage of putting things into his mouth, here are some mommy-tested-and-approved arts and crafts recipes that you can make for absolutely fabulous fun.

I have used these recipes over and over again with my own kids. They are simple to make, and most of the ingredients can be found in your own kitchen cupboard! Many of these arts and crafts projects are as good as or better than store-bought products, but for a fraction of the cost. In fact, some of the projects in this section cost only pennies to make.

So roll up your sleeves and dress for a mess, because you're probably going to get really messy with these activities. And remember, a lot of the fun is in the preparation!

Clay for Baby's Handprints or Footprints

Here's a great idea to make an adorable keepsake for your baby. When this clay hardens, it dries to a nice, matte finish and is great for all sorts of craft projects.

Here's What You Will Need

1 cup baking soda
½ cup cornstarch
1 teaspoon salt
¾ cup water
Large plastic margarine container

In a medium-sized saucepan, mix the baking soda, cornstarch, salt, and water. Heat on high until the mixture begins to boil. Turn heat to low and continue mixing until the mixture becomes thick and creamy and is difficult to stir. Remove from heat. Knead with your hands when cool. Next, place the clay into a large plastic margarine container and flatten out on the top. Have your baby place her hand or foot firmly into the clay to make an imprint. Use a toothpick or pencil to write your baby's name and birth date into the clay. Decorate with stones, shells, marbles, or small mosaic pieces. Let harden for a few days. (Be sure the clay is completely hardened before removing from the container or it may crumble.) If you would like to hang the ornament, use a straw to poke a hole into the top portion of the clay before it has hardened. Tie with a ribbon.

☼ **Other Creative Ideas.** Roll the clay with a rolling pin. Use Christmas cookie cutters to cut shapes into the clay. Use a toothpick or pencil to write your baby's name and date of birth in the clay. Poke a hole in the top of the ornament with a straw and hang on your Christmas tree with a ribbon for a cute, homemade baby's first Christmas ornament!

Jiggle Soap

When I created the recipe for this fun concoction, I had in mind two of the things that my children love the most: bath time and Jell-O. Put the two of them together and here's what I came up with. It's so-ooo cool. This amazing soap wiggles and jiggles and looks just like real Jell-O—but you can't eat it! Kids can play with it in the bathtub, wiggle it, jiggle it, squish it through their fingers, or even wash themselves with it. Bath time will never be the same again.

Here's What You Will Need

1 package Knox gelatin (clear, unflavored)
½ cup hot water
¼ cup liquid bubble bath
Food coloring (optional)

In a small bowl, dissolve the gelatin into the hot water. Next, mix in the bubble bath and stir thoroughly. If you would like colored Jiggle Soap, simply mix in a few drops of food coloring. Refrigerate for at least 4 hours. Cut into cubes. Store in the refrigerator until ready to use.

☼ **Other Creative Ideas.** Cut the Jiggle Soap into cubes and place in a plastic dessert bowl. The kids can squirt some of daddy's shaving cream or some kids' bath foam on top of the soap for a delicious-looking—but inedible—dessert. Great for bath time fun!

Make Fish-in-a-Bag by adding blue food coloring to the soap mixture to make "water," then pour the mixture into a plastic resealable bag. Add a plastic fish or another plastic sea creature to the bag to make Fish-in-a-Bag. Prop the bag upright in your fridge and refrigerate for at least 5 hours. Store in the refrigerator until ready to use. (You will need to triple the recipe to have enough soap to make this project.)

Pour the Jiggle Soap into jars or containers and tie with a ribbon to make a really cool party favor for a child's birthday party. (Store in the refrigerator until ready to use.)

Squishy Bag

When my twins were babies, they loved playing with the Squishy Bag. They would poke it, squish it, and throw it. It's a lot of fun for little ones and costs only pennies to make!

Here's What You Will Need

Glitter, metallic confetti, plastic fish, or other small toys
Large resealable bag
Water or hair gel
Strong tape

Throw some glitter, metallic confetti, or small plastic toys into a large resealable bag. Fill the bag up with water or hair gel and seal it closed with some strong packing tape. Let your little one play with the bag by poking and squishing it.

Added note: You may want to let your child play with the bag outside, just in case it pops open.

☀ **Parental Warning.** If you have placed small items in the bag that may be considered a choking hazard, please supervise your child at all times during play.

Play Dough

Here's a simple play dough recipe that you can make for your child using ingredients that you can find in your own kitchen cupboard. Make sure your child doesn't try to put the play dough into his mouth—this play dough tastes awful, but when has that ever stopped a curious little one!

Here's What You Will Need

2 cups flour
¾ cups salt
4 tablespoons vegetable oil
¾ cups water
Large mixing bowl
Food coloring

Mix the flour, salt, vegetable oil, and water in a large mixing bowl. Mix well and knead with your hands until smooth. If you would like to add color to your play dough, add several drops of food coloring to the water before you add it to the dry ingredients. Store in an airtight container in the refrigerator.

Homemade Bubbles

Children of all ages love bubbles. They are fun to blow, chase around, pop, and catch. The following three bubble recipes are much cheaper than store-bought bubbles, and they work just as well.

Here's What You Will Need

½ cup liquid dish soap
2 cups water
3 teaspoons sugar
Plastic bottles with lids

Mix together the liquid dish soap, water, and sugar. Pour the mixture into the bottles.

Added note: Use nonbreakable plastic bottles to store the bubbles in. You don't want to use glass bottles that might shatter if dropped.

☼ **Other Creative Ideas.** You can make your own bubble wand by tying a pipe cleaner into a small circle, twisting it in the middle, and leaving the remainder of the pipe cleaner straight for the child to hold on to. For a unique bubble wand, try using a plastic strawberry container or the plastic holder from a six-pack of soda.

Monster Bubbles (1)

Here's What You Will Need

1 cup water
½ cup liquid dish soap
⅓ cup glycerin
½ teaspoon sugar
Plastic bottles with lids

To make huge, monster-sized bubbles, mix the water, liquid dish soap, glycerin, and sugar together, stirring well. Place the liquid in nonbreakable plastic bottles. Chill the mixture before use to make the bubbles last even longer.

Monster Bubbles (2)

Here's What You Will Need

3 cups water
1 cup liquid dish soap
¼ cup corn syrup
Plastic bottles with lids

Mix together the water, liquid dish soap, and corn syrup. Stir well. Place in nonbreakable plastic bottles.

Bubble Play

- Let your child blow bubbles through the wand. For the really little ones who tend to put the bubbles into their mouths, have them wave their arm through the air to create bubbles.
- Blow the bubbles for them and have them try to catch them in the air, clap them with their hands, and step on the bubbles to try to break them.
- Give your child the bubble wand and have her try to catch the bubbles in the circle part of the wand before they hit the ground.
- Try blowing the bubbles indoors. Turn on a child-safe fan and let the bubbles blow around the room as your child tries to catch them.
- Be adventurous. Let your child blow bubbles in the bathtub.

Giggle "Goo"

Young children love to get dirty, which is one of the reasons they really enjoy this activity. This goopy substance is a favorite among children, as they can't quite figure out how it works. They can pick it up like a solid, and it will quickly "melt" through their fingers. At times it seems wet, then dry. This "goo" will have your little ones giggling for hours!

Here's What You Will Need

Resealable bag, bowl, or baking sheet
1 cup cornstarch
½ cup water
Food coloring (optional)

You can make this mixture in a bowl or directly in a resealable bag. First, measure the cornstarch and put it into the resealable bag, holding the bag upright. Then add the water and a few drops of food coloring, again holding the bag upright. You can use your fingers or a spoon for mixing. Let your little one dig in with her hands and squish the "goo" through her fingers.

Added note: You may prefer to put the "goo" onto a baking sheet or in a plastic container and let your child play with it in that manner, as opposed to using a resealable bag where the "goo" may spill out. This mixture can be stored in the refrigerator for about a week. To reuse, just add some water and stir. Don't pour the "goo" down the drain, as it will clog.

Icebergs

These mini icebergs will keep your little one as cool as a cucumber on a hot summer's day. A great way to splash the day away!

Here's What You Will Need

Large plastic margarine containers
Water
Food coloring (optional)
Plastic toys (optional)

To make your icebergs, simply fill large plastic margarine containers with water and place in the freezer overnight. To remove the ice, run the containers under warm water. Set your icebergs afloat in a children's pool in the summer, or build a small snow fort or igloo in the winter. (To make huge icebergs, fill up large buckets with water and place outside in the winter to freeze.) You can add food coloring to the water before you freeze it for colored icebergs. Put a small plastic toy in the water before you freeze it. Your child will be pleasantly surprised when the ice melts!

🔆 **Parental Warning.** Parents should always supervise young children when involved in any water play activity.

Wet 'n' Wild Water Play

Little ones love the water. They just can't seem to get enough of it. Here's a terrific way to get a small child slowly used to water play. You'll turn a timid turtle into a frolicking fish in no time at all! Ready . . . set . . . get wet!

Here's What You Will Need

Large garbage bags, old plastic shower curtain, or plastic tablecloth
Hose or sprinkler

Spread some large garbage bags, an old plastic shower curtain, or a plastic tablecloth outside on the lawn. (You may want to tape the garbage bags together with some strong tape.) Turn on a hose or sprinkler, spraying some water directly onto the plastic surface. Sit your child, in her bathing suit, in the middle of the plastic sheet, where she can splash around in the small puddles of water.

🔆 **Parental Warning.** Parents should always supervise young children when involved in any water play activity.

Water Painting

Here are some simple ideas for water play that your child can try outdoors. You'd be surprised how busy these activities will keep her!

- Give your child a jumbo-sized paintbrush and a bucket of water. Have her paint the side of the house, the patio, the car, or whatever she wishes, with water. On a hot sunny day, she will enjoy watching as the water disappears in the hot sun.
- Fill a bucket up with some warm soapy water, give your child some sponges and towels, and let her help you wash your car.
- Let your child wash her tricycle, doll clothes, or other toys using a bucket of warm soapy water.

Miniature Snowman

With this fun activity, your child will have her own miniature version of Frosty the Snowman to play with whenever she likes!

Here's What You Will Need

Clean snow
Bucket
Large garbage bags
Plastic wrap or plastic bags

Have your child help you collect a bucket of clean snow from the backyard. Spread out several garbage bags on the floor, and place the bucket of snow in the middle of the floor. Let your child put on her mittens and make her own miniature snowman. She can even decorate her snowman if she wishes. When she's done, wrap the snowman in some plastic wrap or plastic bags and place in the freezer. It will keep for several weeks.

Snow Play

When it's too cold to play outside, why not bring the fun indoors?

Here's What You Will Need

Large garbage bags or towels
Large bucket

Clean snow

Spoons, pots and pans, cooking utensils, measuring cups,
cookie cutters, sand pails and shovels, spray bottles

Spread several large garbage bags or towels in the middle of the
kitchen floor. Collect a large bucket of clean snow from outside, and place
it on the garbage bags on the floor. Give your child several of the items
listed above. Let him put on his mittens and dig tunnels in the snow and
scoop the snow. He can use the cookie cutters to make "cookies" out of
the snow, simply by pressing the snow into the cookie cutters and removing the snow shapes out onto a plate. (If you like, you can even freeze
the "cookies" in the freezer.) Fill up a plastic squeeze or spray bottle with
some water and food coloring and let your child "paint" the snow.

Alligator Soup

While you're busy cooking dinner in the kitchen, your little one can cook
right along with you, making her own homemade "soup"! (Of course,
this soup is only for alligators, so no tasting!)

Here's What You Will Need

Mixing bowl

Water

Large wooden or plastic spoons

An assortment of spices, rice, or a collection of outdoor goodies,
including sticks, stones, leaves, acorns, and pinecones

Fill a large plastic mixing bowl with water. Give your child some
wooden or plastic spoons to mix with. Have her create her own "soup"
by adding spices, such as salt, pepper, garlic powder, and cinnamon, to
the water. She can have fun stirring and mixing the ingredients together,
making her own soup. Give her any leftovers that you are cooking with
at the time, such as celery, carrots, corn, or rice, to add to her mixture.
Take her on a nature walk in the morning and have her collect an assortment of "ingredients" for her soup, such as leaves, grass, acorns, peb-
bles, or whatever nature has to offer.

Candy Necklace

Here's a craft that is fun to make—and even more fun to eat!

Here's What You Will Need

Licorice whips or string
"O" shaped candies or cereal, pretzels, minidoughnuts (anything
with a hole in it)

Cut licorice whips or string to the length that you would like your
child's necklace to be. Knot at one end. Have your child string several
"O" shaped candies or "O" shaped cereal, such as Fruit Loops or Chee-
rios, onto the string. Tie securely for your child to wear as a deliciously
edible necklace.

Bathtub "Goo"

Okay. It sounds disgusting, and yes, it definitely looks disgusting. But
what does it feel like? Well, let's not go there. But children really do love
it—honest! Your child can cover himself from head to toe in this gooey,
slimy stuff—and the more he uses, the cleaner he'll get!

Here's What You Will Need

1 package Knox gelatin (clear, unflavored)
1½ cups hot water
Food coloring
⅓ cup bubble bath
Plastic wrap
Plastic spiders and rubber worms (optional)

In a small bowl, mix the gelatin with the hot water. Stir briskly with
a fork until dissolved. Next, add several drops of food coloring in the
desired shade. Stir in the bubble bath. For extra-frightful bathtime fun,
mix in some plastic creepy crawlies, such as plastic spiders or rubber
worms. Pour the mixture into a container and cover with plastic wrap.
Refrigerate for about 2 hours. When it reaches a slimy, gooey consis-

tency, it's ready for the tub. Let your child dig in and squish the "goo" between his fingers. Yuck!

Added note: If the mixture has been left in the fridge for too long, it may harden. Simply set it out on the kitchen counter for about an hour until it turns slimy again. You can store the mixture in the fridge for a day or two until you are ready to use it, but keep in mind that you will have to let it sit out to soften and return to its slimy consistency. This mixture washes off with water. Be sure to tell your child not to get it in his eyes, as it may sting.

Pop-Up Soap

Your little one will want to wash himself as clean as he can with this cute soap, just to get to the "pop-up" toy inside!

Here's What You Will Need

Clear natural glycerin soap (available at craft stores)
Glass measuring cup or microwave-safe bowl
Food coloring (optional)
Soap mold or plastic margarine container
Small toys, including small plastic dolls, figurines, rubber ducks, fish, dolphins, and other bathtub toys (do not use heat-sensitive items)
Plastic wrap

Cut soap into 1-inch (2½-centimeter) cubes. Place in a microwave-safe bowl or glass measuring cup and heat on high for about 20 seconds in the microwave. If soap is not completely melted at this time, continue heating at 10- to 15-second intervals until completely melted. (You can also melt the soap by placing it into a glass measuring cup that has been set in a pot of simmering water for about 5 minutes.) For colored soap, mix in a few drops of food coloring. Fill a soap mold or plastic margarine container with about 2 inches (5 centimeters) of the melted soap. Let cool for a few minutes, and then place the bottom portion of a small toy or another object directly in the center of the melted soap, leaving the top portion of the toy to remain outside of the soap, as if it were popping out of it. Place in the refrigerator to cool. When hardened, gently pop the soap out of the mold. Wrap soap in plastic wrap until ready to use.

:ᗄᐧ **Parental Warning.** Be very careful when melting soap. It can be very hot!

Picture Soap

Your child will love taking a bath with her own personal bar of soap, with a picture of herself or a special friend attached!

Here's What You Will Need

Bar of soap with a smooth, flat surface
Photograph or picture
Paraffin wax
Paintbrush

Cut a favorite photo to size, making sure it fits on the smooth surface of the bar of soap. You can also use colorful pictures from magazines or greeting cards or choose a cute cartoon character that your child loves. Using a paintbrush, brush some melted paraffin wax directly onto the flat surface of the soap and on the underside of the photo. Quickly place the picture firmly onto the flat surface of the soap. Next, brush a layer of melted paraffin wax directly over the top of the photo, brushing in one direction only, and covering the entire surface of the picture with the melted wax. When completely hardened, you may want to rub some vegetable oil onto the top surface of the picture with a paper towel to smooth the surface.

:ᗄᐧ **Other Creative Ideas.** Wrap the bars in decorative paper and tie with a pretty ribbon, some raffia, or a bow.

As a special gift for your child to give to a friend, let her choose a favorite photo of herself and her friend together to attach to the bar of soap.

Soap Pump Surprise

One of the things that makes life interesting for the kids around our home are all of the little "surprises" I keep leaving around the house for them to find: small candy treats hidden in their shoes or tucked away in their coat pockets, bread and cheese slices cut into cute little star shapes, and a smiley face or cute little drawing on a steamy bathroom window. Here's an idea to make a little surprise that you can leave around the house for your child— and a great way to get your little one to wash her hands more often, too.

Here's What You Will Need

Clear plastic soap-pump dispenser (clear hand-soap or shampoo dispensers with clear soap inside work the best)
Assorted metallic confetti, shiny beads, buttons, small fabric flowers

Remove the pump from the soap dispenser, and add a small handful of metallic confetti, small beads, bright buttons, or other items that are small enough to fit into the opening of the bottle. Simply shake the bottle a couple of times to see it sparkle. Your child will actually enjoy washing her hands!

Ocean in a Bottle

Your little one will be fascinated by the swirling "ocean waves" when he rolls his Ocean in a Bottle along the floor, rocks it slowly back and forth, or shakes it up to see the magic!

Here's What You Will Need

Clear 2-liter plastic pop bottle with a screw-on lid
2 cups cooking oil
Funnel
Blue food coloring
Glitter, metallic confetti, and sequins
Water

Clean the plastic bottle thoroughly and remove the label. Pour the oil into the plastic bottle, using a funnel. Next, add several drops of blue food coloring and a handful of glitter, metallic confetti, and shiny sequins. Fill to the top with water. Replace the cap, and shake well. Be sure to screw the cap on tightly to avoid any leaks. (You might want to glue the lid on securely with a hot glue gun or some strong glue.) Have your child rock the bottle gently back and forth to make waves, shake it, or roll it along the floor.

Shimmering Bubble Bath

To add some extra sparkle to your child's favorite bubble bath or body wash, simply add some fine, loose glitter to the bubble liquid. She'll be sure to come out "sparkling" clean!

Easy Baby Toys

Don't spend a fortune on expensive baby toys for your baby. Babies don't care how much you spend on toys; in fact, some of the things they will love to play with the most can be found right in your own home! Here are some easy baby toys that you can make from recyclables and other common household items.

Beach and Sandbox Toys

Here are some great ways to recycle your quart- and gallon-size (1-liter and 4-liter) plastic bottles.

Clean the bottles out well, and cut your gallon-size bottle all around, about 6 inches (15 centimeters) from the bottom. Poke a couple holes on opposite sides near the top, attach a rope handle, and you have your sand pail. The remaining piece becomes your funnel. You can cut another gallon-size bottle about 2 inches (5 centimeters) high and poke the bottom full of holes for a sieve. Cut the bottom off your quart-size bottle. Then cut a long U-shaped scoop, sloping your cut up along the sides. (If your bottle comes with a handle, make sure the handle ends up on the top-side of the scoop.) This becomes your shovel. The best part of these toys is that if they get left behind at the beach, you can always make more!

Instant Kite

Take one plastic grocery bag with handles, tie a long length of string to one handle, and *run*!

Free Toy Building Blocks

Thanks to Linda for this Frugal Baby Tip. Here's one recycling tip for turning half-gallon square milk containers into toy blocks. Cut off the pouring end of two rinsed and dried-out milk cartons. Then push the two open ends together, pushing one carton inside the other. This doubles the strength of your new block and closes the ends. These are very lightweight and safe. I started this project while pregnant with my first child, and eight years later we have quite a collection—and it's always a favorite with visiting friends. They make great walls, forts, and cages for kids, as well as cities and roads for small cars.

Wooden Blocks

My children's grandparents made terrific wooden blocks for our kids out of untreated wood they bought at a hardware store. To make these simple wooden blocks for your kids, simply cut the wood into different-sized blocks and sand until smooth. You can also paint these blocks if you wish.

Indoor Sandbox

You can keep your little ones busy on a rainy "stay-in" day by creating an indoor sandbox. All you need is a large plastic dishpan and a 5-pound (2-kilogram) bag of cornmeal or rice for "sand," as well as some spoons, measuring cups, funnels, strainers, and so on. The cornmeal or rice vacuums up quickly and doesn't scratch the floor.

Baby's Discovery Board

Place a bulletin board or sheet of cork on the wall near (but out of reach of) your baby's bed or changing table. When objects and colors begin to fascinate your newborn, you can attach different objects and pictures to the Discovery Board for your baby to look at. Later, this can be a place to display your toddler's artwork. Watch out for the pins, though!

Things to Save Throughout the Year

The following is a list of things that you can collect and save throughout the year to make some terrific free toys, games, and other fun and creative play items for your baby—a great way to recycle!

Drums
- Empty coffee cans
- Pots and pans
- Wooden spoons

Shakers
- Empty margarine container, plastic bottle, or empty film container filled with dried rice or uncooked pasta

Tambourine
- Aluminum pie plate

Wrist Bells
- Several small gold or silver jingle bells strung together on an elastic band to make jingle bell bracelets, which can be tied around a child's wrist

Water Toys
- Turkey baster
- Measuring cups and funnels for pouring
- Squirt and spray bottles
- Sieve
- Styrofoam meat trays for boats

Educational Toys
- Cups for stacking
- Socks for matching
- Buttons for sorting
- Junk mail and old Christmas and birthday cards for sorting and opening

Games
- Plastic soda bottles for bowling pins
- Plastic lids and paper plates for Frisbees

Pretend Play
- Large cardboard appliance box for a play fort
- Smaller cardboard boxes to make cars, buses, and trains
- Paper bags and socks for puppets
- Old jewelry, shoes, scarves, hats, dresses, etc., for dress-up play
- White jacket, bandages, and Popsicle sticks for a doctor's kit

The "Mess" Factor

Arts and crafts time with your little one can get very messy. That's just part of the fun! Here are some great ideas to help reduce the "mess" factor.

Art Smock

Make a full-body smock to cover your child's clothing by cutting a hole in the top of a garbage bag for his head and two holes at each side of the garbage bag for his arms. An oversized T-shirt can also be used to protect your child's clothing.

Great Floor Savers

1. Cut and open up garbage bags at the seams, and place them under your child's worktable or high chair to protect your floors from accidental spills.

2. Use old towels, drop cloths, or sheets of plastic to place under your child's work area. An old shower curtain or plastic tablecloth also works well to protect the floors from spills.

Shaving Cream Clean-Up

For a fun way to get your child's hands clean after finger painting or other messy art projects, give your child a squirt of daddy's shaving cream and have her rub it into her hands and arms to "play" with it to get clean. This is a fun way for your child to get clean and makes mommy and daddy's job much easier as well!

From the Author

We are anticipating possible future editions of this book. Have you discovered any free items for new or expecting parents that are not listed in our book that are currently valid? Does your company have free offers that you would like to make available to new or expecting parents? Companies, government agencies, and support groups are invited to submit items for consideration in our next revised edition. A description and actual sample of your offer is best for us to review it and write up an accurate description. Please contact the author by E-mail or regular mail with your submission. (See the Introduction for contact information.)

When submitting your offer, keep in mind that we want to keep our offers free. Your offer must be free, with no obligation to buy anything. It must be available to residents of the United States, Canada, or both, and it must be related to parenting, babies, or child care.

About the Author

Sue Hannah is the mother of three children, Kayla, aged 4, and twins Shane and Katie, 1½ years of age. Her writing has appeared in various magazines in the United States and Canada, including *U.S. Kids*, *Alive Journal of Health and Nutrition*, *Schooldays*, and *What's Up Kids?*, as well as her local newspaper, *The Cambridge Times*. She is also the author of an upcoming children's craft book titled *Crafty Concoctions*.